LAZARUS LAUGHED

A Play for an Imaginative Theatre

by
Eugene O'Neill

Contents

Characters and Settings

Characters:

LAZARUS OF BETHANY

HIS FATHER

HIS MOTHER

MARTHA; MARY, *his sisters*

MIRIAM, *his wife*

SEVEN GUESTS, *neighbors of Lazarus*

CHORUS OF OLD MEN

AN ORTHODOX PRIEST

CHORUS OF LAZARUS' FOLLOWERS

A CENTURION

GAIUS CALIGULA

CRASSUS, *a Roman General*

CHORUS OF GREEKS

SEVEN CITIZENS OF ATHENS

CHORUS OF ROMAN SENATORS

SEVEN SENATORS

CHORUS OF LEGIONARIES

FLAVIUS, *a centurion*

MARCELLUS, *a patrician*

Lazarus Laughed

CHORUS OF THE GUARD

TIBERIUS CÆSAR

POMPEIA

CHORUS OF YOUTHS AND GIRLS

CHORUS OF THE ROMAN POPULACE

CROWDS

Settings:

ACT ONE

SCENE I: Lazarus' home in Bethany--a short time after the miracle.

SCENE II: Months later. Outside the House of Laughter in Bethany. Late evening.

ACT TWO

SCENE I: A street in Athens. A night months later.

SCENE II: A temple immediately inside the walls of Rome. Midnight. Months later.

ACT THREE

SCENE I: Garden of Tiberius' palace. A night a few days later.

SCENE II: Inside the palace. Immediately after.

ACT FOUR

SCENE I: The same. A while after.

SCENE II: Interior of a Roman theatre. Dawn of the same night.

ACT ONE

SCENE ONE

SCENE--*Exterior and interior of Lazarus' home at Bethany. The main room at the front end of the house is shown--a long, low-ceilinged, sparely furnished chamber, with white walls gray in the fading daylight that enters from three small windows at the left. To the left of center several long tables placed lengthwise to the width of the room, around which many chairs for guests have been placed. In the rear wall, right, a door leading into the rest of the house. On the left, a doorway opening on a road where a crowd of men has gathered. On the right, another doorway leading to the yard where there is a crowd of women.*

Inside the house, on the men's side, seven male Guests are grouped by the door, watching Lazarus with frightened awe, talking hesitantly in low whispers. The Chorus of Old Men, seven in number, is drawn up in a crescent, in the far corner, right, facing Lazarus.

(All of these people are masked in accordance with the following scheme: There are seven periods of life shown: Boyhood [or Girlhood], Youth, Young Manhood [or Womanhood], Manhood [or Womanhood], Middle Age, Maturity and Old Age; and each of these periods is represented by seven different masks of general types of character as follows: The Simple, Ignorant; the Happy, Eager; the Self-Tortured, Introspective; the Proud, Self-Reliant; the Servile, Hypocritical; the Revengeful, Cruel; the Sorrowful, Resigned. Thus in each crowd [this includes among the men the Seven Guests who are composed of one male of each period-type as period one--type one, period two--type two, and so on up to period seven--type seven] there are forty-nine different combinations of period and type. Each type has

a distinct predominant color for its costumes which varies in kind according to its period. The masks of the Chorus of Old Men are double the size of the others. They are all seven in the Sorrowful, Resigned type of Old Age.)

On a raised platform at the middle of the one table placed lengthwise at center sits Lazarus, his head haloed and his body illumined by a soft radiance as of tiny phosphorescent flames.

Lazarus, freed now from the fear of death, wears no mask.

In appearance Lazarus is tall and powerful, about fifty years of age, with a mass of gray-black hair and a heavy beard. His face recalls that of a statue of a divinity of Ancient Greece in its general structure and particularly in its quality of detached serenity. It is dark-complected, ruddy and brown, the color of rich earth upturned by the plow, calm but furrowed deep with the marks of former suffering endured with a grim fortitude that had never softened into resignation. His forehead is broad and noble, his eyes black and deep-set. Just now he is staring straight before him as if his vision were still fixed beyond life.

Kneeling beside him with bowed heads are his wife, Miriam, his sisters, Martha and Mary, and his Father and Mother.

Miriam is a slender, delicate woman of thirty-five, dressed in deep black, who holds one of his hands in both of hers, and keeps her lips pressed to it. The upper part of her face is covered by a mask which conceals her forehead, eyes and nose, but leaves her mouth revealed. The mask is the pure pallor of marble, the expression that of a statue of Woman, of her eternal acceptance of the compulsion of motherhood, the inevitable cycle of love into pain into joy and new love into separation and pain again and the loneliness of age. The eyes of the mask are almost closed. Their gaze turns within, oblivious to the life outside, as they dream down on the child forever in memory at her breast. The mouth of Miriam is sensitive and sad, tender with an eager, understanding smile of self-forgetful love, the lips still fresh and young. Her skin, in contrast to the mask, is sunburned and earth-colored like that of Lazarus. Martha, Mary and the two parents all wear full masks which broadly reproduce their own characters. Martha is a buxom middle-aged housewife, plain and pleasant. Mary is young and pretty, nervous and high-strung. The Father is a small, thin, feeble old man of over eighty, meek and pious. The Mother is tall and stout, over sixty-five, a gentle, simple woman.

All the masks of these Jews of the first two scenes of the play are pronouncedly Semitic.

A background of twilight sky. A dissolving touch of sunset still lingers on the horizon.

It is some time after the miracle and Jesus has gone away.

CHORUS OF OLD MEN--(*in a quavering rising and falling chant--their arms outstretched toward Lazarus*)

Jesus wept!
Behold how he loved him!
He that liveth,
He that believeth,
Shall never die!

CROWD--(*on either side of house, echo the chant*)

He that believeth
Shall never die!
Lazarus, come forth!

FIRST GUEST--(*a Simple Boy--in a frightened whisper after a pause of dead silence*) That strange light seems to come from within him! (*with awe*) Think of it! For four days he lay in the tomb! (*turns away with a shudder*)

SECOND GUEST--(*a Happy Youth--with reassuring conviction*) It is a holy light. It came from Jesus.

FIFTH GUEST--(*an Envious, Middle-Aged Man*) Maybe if the truth were known, our friend there never really died at all!

FOURTH GUEST--(*a Defiant Man, indignantly*) Do you doubt the miracle? I tell you I was here in this house when Lazarus died!

SEVENTH GUEST--(*an Aged, Sorrowful Man*) And I used to visit him every day. He knew himself his hour was near.

FOURTH GUEST--He wished for death! He said to me one day: "I have known my fill of life and the sorrow of living. Soon I shall know

9

peace." And he smiled. It was the first time I had seen him smile in years.

THIRD GUEST--(*a Self-Tortured Man--gloomily*) Yes, of late years his life had been one long misfortune. One after another his children died--

SIXTH GUEST--(*a Mature Man with a cruel face--with a harsh laugh*) They were all girls. Lazarus had no luck.

SEVENTH GUEST--The last was a boy, the one that died at birth. You are forgetting him.

THIRD GUEST--Lazarus could never forget. Not only did his son die but Miriam could never bear him more children.

FIFTH GUEST--(*practically*) But he could not blame bad luck for everything. Take the loss of his father's wealth since he took over the management. That was his own doing. He was a bad farmer, a poor breeder of sheep, and a bargainer so easy to cheat it hurt one's conscience to trade with him!

SIXTH GUEST--(*with a sneer--maliciously*) You should know best about that! (*a suppressed laugh from those around him*)

FIRST GUEST--(*who has been gazing at Lazarus--softly*) Ssssh! Look at his face! (*They all stare. A pause.*)

SECOND GUEST--(*with wondering awe*) Do you remember him, neighbors, before he died? He used to be pale even when he worked in the fields. Now he seems as brown as one who has labored in the earth all day in a vineyard beneath the hot sun! (*a pause*)

FOURTH GUEST--The whole look of his face has changed. He is like a stranger from a far land. There is no longer any sorrow in his eyes. They must have forgotten sorrow in the grave.

FIFTH GUEST--(*grumblingly*) I thought we were invited here to eat-- and all we do is stand and gape at him!

FOURTH GUEST--(*sternly*) Be silent! We are waiting for him to speak.

THIRD GUEST--(*impressively*) He did speak once. And he laughed!

ALL THE GUESTS--(*amazed and incredulous*) Laughed?

THIRD GUEST--(*importantly*) Laughed! I heard him! It was a moment after the miracle--

MIRIAM--(*her voice, rich with sorrow, exultant now*) Jesus cried, "Lazarus, come forth!" (*She kisses his hand. He makes a slight movement, a stirring in his vision. The Guests stare. A frightened pause.*)

FIFTH GUEST--(*nudging the Second--uneasily*) Go on with your story!

THIRD GUEST--Just as he appeared in the opening of the tomb, wrapped in his shroud--

SECOND GUEST--(*excitedly--interrupting*) My heart stopped! I fell on my face! And all the women screamed! (*sceptically*) You must have sharp ears to have heard him laugh in that uproar!

THIRD GUEST--I helped to pry away the stone so I was right beside him. I found myself kneeling, but between my fingers I watched Jesus and Lazarus. Jesus looked into his face for what seemed a long time and suddenly Lazarus said "Yes" as if he were answering a question in Jesus' eyes.

ALL THE GUESTS--(*mystified*) Yes? What could he mean by yes?

THIRD GUEST--Then Jesus smiled sadly but with tenderness, as one who from a distance of years of sorrow remembers happiness. And then Lazarus knelt and kissed Jesus' feet and both of them smiled and Jesus blessed him and called him "My Brother" and went away; and Lazarus, looking after Him, began to laugh softly like a man in love with God! Such a laugh I never heard! It made my ears drunk! It was like wine! And though I was half-dead with fright I found myself laughing, too!

MIRIAM--(*with a beseeching summons*) Lazarus, come forth!

CHORUS--(*chanting*) Lazarus! Come forth!

CROWD--(*on either side of the house--echoing the chant*) Come forth! Come forth!

LAZARUS--(*suddenly in a deep voice--with a wonderful exultant acceptance in it*) Yes! (*The Guests in the room, the Crowds outside all cry out in fear and joy and fall on their knees.*)

CHORUS--(*chanting exultantly*)

The stone is taken away!
The spirit is loosed!
The soul let go!

LAZARUS--(*rising and looking around him at everyone and every-thing--with an all-embracing love--gently*) Yes! (*His family and the Guests in the room now throng about Lazarus to embrace him. The Crowds of men and women on each side push into the room to stare at him. He is in the arms of his Mother and Miriam while his Sisters and Father kiss and press his hands. The five are half hysterical with relief and joy, sobbing and laughing.*)

FATHER--My son is reborn to me!

CHORUS--Hosannah!

ALL--(*with a great shout*) Hosannah!

FATHER--Let us rejoice! Eat and drink! Draw up your chairs, friends! Music! Bring wine! (*Music begins in the room off right, rear--a festive dance tune. The company sit down in their places, the Father and Mother at Lazarus' right and left, Miriam next to the Mother, Martha and Mary beside the Father. But Lazarus remains standing. And the Chorus of Old Men remain in their formation at the rear. Wine is poured and all raise their goblets toward Lazarus--then suddenly they stop, the music dies out, and an awed and frightened stillness prevails, for Lazarus is a strange, majestic figure whose understanding smile seems terrible and enigmatic to them.*)

FATHER--(*pathetically uneasy*) You frighten us, my son. You are strange--standing there--(*In the midst of a silence more awkward than before he rises to his feet, goblet in hand--forcing his voice, falter-ingly*) A toast, neighbors!

CHORUS--(*in a forced echo*) A toast!

ALL--(*echoing them*) A toast!

FATHER--To my son, Lazarus, whom a blessed miracle has brought back from death!

LAZARUS--(*suddenly laughing softly out of his vision, as if to him-self, and speaking with a strange unearthly calm in a voice that is like a loving whisper of hope and confidence*) No! There is no death! (*A *moment's pause. The people remain with goblets uplifted, staring at him. Then all repeat after him questioningly and frightenedly*)

ALL--There--is--no--death?

SIXTH GUEST--(*suddenly blurts out the question which is in the minds of all*) What did you find beyond there, Lazarus? (*a pause of silence*)

LAZARUS--(*smiles gently and speaks as if to a group of inquisitive children*) O Curious Greedy Ones, is not one world in which you know not how to live enough for you?

SIXTH GUEST--(*emboldened*) Why did you say yes, Lazarus?

FOURTH GUEST--Why did you laugh?

ALL THE GUESTS--(*with insistent curiosity but in low awed tones*) What is beyond there, Lazarus?

CHORUS--(*in a low murmur*) What is beyond there? What is beyond?

CROWD--(*carrying the question falteringly back into silence*) What is beyond?

LAZARUS--(*suddenly again--now in a voice of loving exaltation*) There is only life! I heard the heart of Jesus laughing in my heart; "There is Eternal Life in No," it said, "and there is the same Eternal Life in Yes! Death is the fear between!" And my heart reborn to love of life cried "Yes!" and I laughed in the laughter of God! (*He begins to laugh, softly at first--a laugh so full of a complete acceptance of life, a profound assertion of joy in living, so devoid of all self-consciousness or fear, that it is like a great bird song triumphant in depths of sky, proud and powerful, infectious with love, casting on the listener an enthralling spell. The Crowd in the room are caught by it. Glancing sideways at one another, smiling foolishly and self-consciously, at first they hesitate, plainly holding themselves in for fear of what the next one will think.*)

CHORUS--(*in a chanting murmur*)

Lazarus laughs!
Our hearts grow happy!
Laughter like music!
The wind laughs!
The sea laughs!

13

Lazarus Laughed

Spring laughs from the earth!
Summer laughs in the air!
Lazarus laughs!

LAZARUS--(*on a final note of compelling exultation*) Laugh! Laugh with me! Death is dead! Fear is no more! There is only life! There is only laughter!

CHORUS--(*chanting exultingly now*)

Laugh! Laugh!
Laugh with Lazarus!
Fear is no more!
There is no death!

(*They laugh in a rhythmic cadence dominated by the laughter of Lazarus.*)

CROWD--(*who, gradually, joining in by groups or one by one-- including Lazarus' family with the exception of Miriam, who does not laugh but watches and listens to his laughter with a tender smile of being happy in his happiness--have now all begun to laugh in rhythm with the Chorus--in a great, full-throated pœan as the laughter of Lazarus rises higher and higher*)

Laugh! Laugh!
Fear is no more!
There is no death!

CHORUS--

Laugh! Laugh!
There is only life!
There is only laughter!
Fear is no more!
Death is dead!

CROWD--(*in a rhythmic echo*)

Laugh! Laugh!
Death is dead!
There is only laughter!

(*The room rocks, the air outside throbs with the rhythmic beat of their liberated laughter--still a bit uncertain of its freedom, harsh, discor-*

dant, frenzied, desperate and drunken, but dominated and inspired by the high, free, aspiring, exulting laughter of Lazarus.)

(*Curtain*)

SCENE TWO

SCENE--*Some months later. Exterior of Lazarus' home in Bethany, now known as the House of Laughter. It is a clear bright night, the sky sparkling with stars. At the extreme front is a road. Between this and the house is a small raised terrace. The house is low, of one story only, its walls white. Four windows are visible with a closed door in the middle of the wall. Steps lead up to this door, and to the left of door a flight of stairs goes up to the balustraded roof. The windows shine brilliantly with the flickering light of many candles which gives them a throbbing star-like effect. From within comes the sound of flutes and dance music. The dancers can be seen whirling swiftly by the windows. There is continually an overtone of singing laughter emphasizing the pulsing rhythm of the dance.*

On the road in the foreground, at left and right, two separate groups of Jews are gathered. They are not divided according to sex as in the previous scene. Each is composed about equally of men and women, forty-nine in each, masked and costumed as before. It is religious belief that now divides them. The adherents of Jesus, the Nazarenes, among whom may be noted Martha and Mary, are on the left; the Orthodox, among whom are Lazarus' Father and Mother and a Priest, are at right. Between the two hostile groups is the same Chorus of Old Men, in a formation like a spearhead, whose point is placed at the foot of the steps leading to the terrace. All these people are staring fascinatedly at the house, listening entranced, their feet moving, their bodies swaying to the music's beat, stiffly, constrainedly, compelled against their wills. Then the music suddenly stops and the chant of youthful voices is heard:

FOLLOWERS OF LAZARUS--(*from within the house*)

Laugh! Laugh!
There is only life!
There is only laughter!

CHORUS OF OLD MEN--(*as if they were subjects moved by hypnotic suggestion--miserably and discordantly*)

Ha-ha-ha-ha!
There is only laughter!
Ha-ha--

CROWD--(*in the same manner*) Ha-ha--

MARY--Ha--(*then frantically--half-weeping with indignant rage--to the Nazarenes*) Stop! Oh, how can we laugh! We are betraying Jesus! My brother Lazarus has become a devil!

THE ORTHODOX PRIEST--(*His mask is that of a religious fanatic. He is sixty or so.*) Ha--ha--(*tearing his beard and stamping with rage*) Stop it, you fools! It is a foul sin in the sight of Jehovah! Why do you come here every night to listen and watch their abominations? The Lord God will punish you!

MARY--(*echoing him--to her people*) Jesus will never forgive you!

THE PRIEST--(*angrily*) Jesus? (*He turns to look at the Nazarenes disdainfully and spits on the ground insultingly. The members of the two groups begin to glare at each other. The Chorus falls back, three on each side, leaving one neutral figure before the steps. The Priest goes on tauntingly.*) Did you hear her, friends? These renegade Nazarenes will soon deny they are Jews at all! They will begin to worship in filthy idolatry the sun and stars and man's body--as Lazarus in there, (*points to the house*) the disciple of their Jesus, has so well set them the example! (*This is followed by an outburst of insulting shouts of accusation and denial from both sides.*)

A NAZARENE--(*the Fourth Guest of Scene One*) You lie! Lazarus is no disciple! He is a traitor to Jesus! We scorn him!

PRIEST--(*sneeringly*) But your pretended Messiah did not scorn him. According to your stupid lies, he raised him from the dead! And answer me, has your Jesus ever denied Lazarus, or denounced his laughter? No! No doubt he is laughing, too, at all you credulous fools--

17

for if Lazarus is not his disciple, in the matter of the false miracle he was his accomplice! (*This provokes a furious protest from the Nazarenes and insulting hoots and jeers from the Orthodox, penetrated by a piercing scream from Lazarus' Mother, who, crushed in the crowd, sinks fainting to the ground. The Father bends over her. The group of the Orthodox falls back from them. With frightened cries Martha and Mary run from the group of Nazarenes and kneel beside her.*)

FATHER--(*pitifully*) Rachel! Darling! Speak to me!

MARTHA--(*practically*) She has only fainted.

MARY--She is opening her eyes! Mother, dear!

MOTHER--(*weakly*) Did I fall? (*recognizing Martha and Mary*) Martha--and Mary--my dear ones! (*They embrace her, weeping.*) I have not kissed you since you left home to follow that Jesus--Oh, if we were only at home again--and if, also, my poor boy, Lazarus--(*She sobs.*)

FATHER--(*gruffly*) You must not speak of him!

MARTHA--Do not worry your head about Lazarus. He is not worth it!

MARY--(*with surprising vindictiveness*) He is accursed! He has betrayed our Lord!

PRIEST--(*to those around him--mockingly*) Do you hear? They already call the Nazarene "Lord!" A Lord who is in the common prison at Jerusalem, I heard today! A fine Lord whom our High Priests have had arrested like a thief!

MARY--(*with fanatic fervor*) He is a king! Whenever He chooses He will gather a great army and He will seize His kingdom and all who deny Him shall be crucified!

PRIEST--(*tauntingly*) Now their jail-bird is a king, no less! Soon they will make him a god, as the Romans do their Cæsars!

MARY--(*her eyes flashing*) He is the Messiah!

PRIEST--(*furiously*) The Messiah! May Jehovah smite you in your lies! Step back among your kind! You defile us! (*As she stands defiantly he appeals to the Father.*) Have you no authority? She called him the Messiah--that common beggar, that tramp! Curse her!

FATHER--(*confused, pitifully harried, collecting his forces*) Wait! Go back, Mary! You chose to follow that impostor--

MARY--(*defiantly*) The Messiah!

MARTHA--(*trying to calm her*) Ssssh! Remember he is our father!

MARY--(*fanatically*) I deny him! I deny all who deny Jesus!

MOTHER--(*tearfully*) And me, darling?

MARY--You must come to us, Mother! You must believe in Jesus and leave all to follow Him!

FATHER--(*enraged*) So! You want to steal your mother away, to leave me lonely in my old age! You are an unnatural daughter! I disown you! Go, before I curse--

MOTHER--(*beseechingly*) Father!

MARTHA--(*pulling Mary away*) Mary! Jesus teaches to be kind.

MARY--(*hysterically*) He teaches to give up all and follow Him! I want to give Him everything! I want my father to curse me!

FATHER--(*frenziedly*) Then I do curse you! No--not you--but the devil in you! And the devil in Martha! And the great mocking devil that dwells in Lazarus and laughs from his mouth! I curse these devils and that Prince of Devils, that false prophet, Jesus! It is he who has brought division to my home and many homes that were happy before. I curse him! I curse the day he called my good son, Lazarus, from the grave to walk again with a devil inside him! It was not my son who came back but a devil! My son is dead! And you, my daughters, are dead! I am the father only of devils! (*His voice has risen to a wailing lament.*) My children are dead!

LAZARUS--(*His voice rings from within the house in exultant denial.*) Death is dead! There is only laughter! (*He laughs.*)

(*The voices of all his Followers echo his laughter. They pour in a laughing rout from the doorway onto the terrace. At the same moment the Chorus of Followers appears on the roof and forms along the balustrade, facing front.*

(*These Followers of Lazarus, forty-nine in number, composed about equally of both sexes, wear a mask that, while recognizably Jewish, is a Lazarus mask, resembling him in its expression of fearless faith in life, the mouth shaped by laughter. The Chorus of Followers, seven in number, all men, have identical masks of double size, as before. The Period of all these masks is anywhere between Youth and Manhood [or Womanhood].*

(*The music continues to come from within. Laughing, the Followers dance to it in weaving patterns on the terrace. They are dressed in bright-colored diaphanous robes. Their chorused laughter, now high and clear, now dying to a humming murmur, stresses the rhythmic flow of the dance.*)

CHORUS OF FOLLOWERS--

Laugh! Laugh!
There is no death!
There is only laughter!

FOLLOWERS--

There is only laughter!
Death is dead!
Laugh! Laugh!

CROWD--(*The two groups of Nazarenes and Orthodox, on the appearance of the Followers, immediately forget their differences and form into one mob, led by their Chorus of Old Men, whose jeering howls they echo as one voice.*) Yaah! Yaah! Yaah! (*But they cannot keep it up. The music and laughter rise above their hooting. They fall into silence. Then they again begin to feel impelled by the rhythm and laughter, their feet move, their bodies sway. Their lips quiver, their mouths open as if to laugh. Their Chorus of Old Men are the first to be affected. It is as if this reaction were transmitted through the Chorus to the Crowd.*)

PRIEST--(*his mouth twitching--fighting against the compulsion in him--stammers*) Brothers--listen--we must unite--in one cause--to--stamp out--this abomination! (*It is as if he can no longer control his speech. He presses his hand over his mouth convulsively.*)

AN AGED ORTHODOX JEW--(*the Seventh Guest of Scene One--starts to harangue the crowd. He fights the spell but cannot control his jerking body nor his ghastly, spasmodic laughter.*) Neighbors! Our young people are corrupted! They are leaving our farms--to dance and sing! To laugh! Ha--! Laugh at everything! Ha-ha--! (*He struggles desperately to control himself.*)

CHORUS OF OLD MEN--(*a barking laugh forced from them*) Ha-ha--!

CROWD--(*echoing this*) Ha-ha--!

THE AGED JEW--They have no respect for life! When I said in kindness, "You must go back to work," they laughed at me! Ha--! "We desire joy. We go to Lazarus," they said--and left my fields! I begged them to stay--with tears in my eyes! I even offered them more money! They laughed! "What is money? Can the heart eat gold?" They laughed at money! Ha-ha--! (*He chokes with exasperated rage.*)

CHORUS OF OLD MEN--(*echoing him*) Ha-ha--!

CROWD--(*echoing the Chorus*) Ha-ha--!

AGED JEW--(*shaking his fist at Lazarus' Followers*) That loafer taught them that! They come to him and work for nothing! For nothing! And they are glad, these undutiful ones! While they sow, they dance! They sing to the earth when they are plowing! They tend his flocks and laugh toward the sun! Ha-ha-ha--! (*He struggles again.*)

CHORUS OF OLD MEN--(*as before*) Ha-ha-ha--

CROWD--(*as before*) Ha-ha-ha--

AGED JEW--How can we compete with labor for laughter! We will have no harvest. There will be no food! Our children will starve! Our race will perish! And he will laugh! Ha-ha-ha-ha! (*He howls with furious, uncontained laughter.*)

CHORUS OF OLD MEN--(*echoing his tone*) Our children will starve! Our race will perish! Lazarus laughs! Ha-ha-ha-ha! Ha-ha-ha-ha!

CROWD--(*as before*) Ha-ha-ha-ha! Ha-ha-ha-ha! (*Their former distinctions of Nazarenes and Orthodox are now entirely forgotten. The members of Lazarus' family are grouped in the center as if nothing had ever happened to separate them. The Chorus of Old Men is again joined in its spearhead formation at the stairs. Apparent first in this Chorus, a queer excitement begins to pervade this mob. They begin to weave in and out, clasping each other's hands now and then, moving mechanically in jerky steps to the music in a grotesque sort of marionettes' country dance. At first this is slow but it momentarily becomes more hectic and peculiar. They raise clenched fists or hands distended into threatening talons. Their voices sound thick and harsh and animal-like with anger as they mutter and growl, each one aloud to himself or herself.*)

CHORUS OF OLD MEN--(*threateningly, gradually rising to hatred*)

Hear them laugh!
See them dance!
Shameless! Wanton!
Dirty! Evil!
Infamous! Bestial!
Madness! Blood!
Adultery! Murder!
We burn!
We kill!
We crucify!
Death! Death!
Beware, Lazarus!

(*this last in a wild frenzy*)

CROWD--(*frenziedly*)

Beware, Lazarus!
We burn! We kill!
We crucify!
Death! Death!

(*They crowd toward the gateway, their arms stretched out as if demanding Lazarus for a sacrificial victim. Meanwhile they never cease to hop up and down, to mill around, to twist their bodies toward and away from each other in bestial parody of the dance of the Followers.*

(*The tall figure of Lazarus, dressed in a white robe, suddenly appears on the roof of the house. He stands at the balustrade in the middle of the Chorus. Beside him, a little behind, Miriam appears dressed in black, her face upturned, her lips praying. She appears to have grown older, to be forty now. Lazarus' body is softly illumined by its inner light. The change in him is marked. He seems ten years younger, at the prime of forty. His body has become less angular and stiff. His movements are graceful and pliant. The change is even more noticeable in his face, which has filled out, become purer in outline, more distinctly*

Grecian. His complexion is the red-brown of rich earth, the gray in his black, curly beard has almost disappeared.

(*He makes a sign and the music ceases. His Followers remain fixed in their dancing attitudes like figures in a frieze. Each member of the mob remains frozen in a distorted posture. He stares down at the mob pityingly, his face calm.*)

LAZARUS--(*speaks amid a profound silence. His voice releases his own dancers and the mob from their fixed attitudes. The music begins to play again within the house, very soft and barely audible, swelling up and down like the sound of an organ from a distant church.*) You laugh, but your laughter is guilty! It laughs a hyena laughter, spotted, howling its hungry fear of life! That day I returned did I not tell you your fear was no more, that there is no death? You believed then--for a moment! You laughed--discordantly, hoarsely, but with a groping toward joy. What! Have you so soon forgotten, that now your laughter curses life again as of old? (*He pauses--then sadly*) That is your tragedy! You forget! You forget the God in you! You wish to forget! Remembrance would imply the high duty to live as a son of God-- generously!--with love!--with pride!--with laughter! This is too glorious a victory for you, too terrible a loneliness! Easier to forget, to become only a man, the son of a woman, to hide from life against her breast, to whimper your fear to her resigned heart and be comforted by her resignation! To live by denying life! (*then exhortingly*) Why are your eyes always either fixed on the ground in weariness of thought, or watching one another with suspicion? Throw your gaze upward! To Eternal Life! To the fearless and deathless! The everlasting! To the stars! (*He stretches out his arms to the sky--then suddenly points.*) See! A new star has appeared! It is the one that shone over Bethlehem! (*His voice becomes a little bitter and mocking.*) The Master of Peace and Love has departed this earth. Let all stars be for you henceforth symbols of Saviors--Sons of God who appeared on worlds like ours to tell the saving truth to ears like yours, inexorably deaf! (*then exaltedly*) But the greatness of Saviors is that they may not save! The greatness of Man is that no god can save him--until he becomes a god! (*He stares up at the stars, rapt in contemplation, oblivious to all around him now.*

(*Rapidly approaching from the left a man's voice jarring in high-pitched cruel laughter is heard. They all listen, huddled together like sheep.*)

23

MESSENGER--(*The Third Guest of Scene One rushes in breathlessly, shouting*) The Nazarene has been crucified!

PRIEST--(*with fierce triumph*) Jehovah is avenged! Hosannah!

ORTHODOX--Hosannah! The false prophet is dead! The pretended Messiah is dead! (*They jump and dance, embracing one another. The Nazarenes stand paralyzed and stunned. The two groups mechanically separate to right and left again, the Chorus of Old Men dividing itself as before.*)

MARY--(*in a frenzy of grief*) Do not believe him! Jesus could not die! (*But at this moment a Nazarene youth, exhausted by grief and tears, staggers in from the left.*)

MESSENGER--(*Second Guest of Scene One*) Jesus is dead! Our Lord is murdered! (*He sinks on his knees sobbing. All the Nazarenes do likewise, wailing, rending their garments, tearing their hair, some even beating their heads on the ground in the agony of their despair.*)

MARY--(*insane with rage now*) They have murdered Him! (*to her Followers--savagely*) An eye for an eye! Avenge the Master! (*Their frenzy of grief turned into rage, the Nazarenes leap to their feet threateningly. Concealed swords and knives are brought out by both sides.*)

MIRIAM--(*leaning over the balustrade--in a voice of entreaty*) Mary! Brothers! (*But none heed her or seem to see her. Lazarus and his Followers remain oblivious to men, arms up-stretched toward the stars, their heads thrown back.*)

MARY--(*wildly*) Vengeance! Death to His murderers!

PRIEST--(*fiercely to his Followers*) Death to the Nazarenes! (*With cries of rage the two groups rush on one another. There is a confused tumult of yells, groans, curses, the shrieks of women, the sounds of blows as they meet in a pushing, whirling, struggling mass in which individual figures are indistinguishable. Knives and swords flash above the heads of the mass, hands in every tense attitude of striking, clutching, tearing are seen upraised. As the fight is at its height a Roman Centurion and a squad of eight Soldiers come tramping up at the double-quick. They all are masked. These Roman masks now and henceforth in the play are carried out according to the same formula of Seven Periods, Seven Types, as those of the Jews seen previously, except that the basis of each face is Roman--heavy, domineering, self-*

*complacent, the face of a confident dominant race. The Centurion dif-
fers from his soldiers only in being more individualized. He is middle-
aged, his soldiers belong to the Period of Manhood. All are of the
Simple, Ignorant Type.*)

CENTURION--(*shouts commandingly*) Disperse! (*But no one hears
him--with angry disgust to his Soldiers*) Charge! Cut them down! (*The
Soldiers form a wedge and charge with a shout. They soon find it nec-
essary to use their swords, and strike down everyone in their way.*)

MIRIAM--Mercy, Romans! (*As they pay no attention to her, in des-
peration she embraces Lazarus beseechingly, forcing his attention
back to earth.*) Lazarus! Mercy!

LAZARUS--(*looks down upon the struggling mass and cries in a ringing voice*) Hold! (*Each person stands transfixed, frozen in the last
movement, even the Roman Soldiers and the Centurion himself. Ten
dead and mortally wounded lie on the ground, trampled by the feet of
friend and foe alike. Lazarus looks at the Crowd. To each he seems to
look at him or her alone. His eyes are accusing and stern. As one
head, the heads of all are averted. Even the Centurion stares at the
ground humbly, in spite of himself. Finally Lazarus speaks in a voice
of infinite disdain.*) Sometimes it is hard to laugh--even *at* men! (*He
turns his eyes from them, staring straight before him. This seems to
release them from their fixed positions. The Nazarenes and the Orthodox separate and slink guiltily apart. The Chorus of Old Men forms
again, the apex at the center of the steps as before. A low wail of lamentation arises from them. The two crowds of Nazarenes and Orthodox
echo this.*)

CHORUS OF OLD MEN--(*in a wailing chant*)

Woe unto Israel!
Woe unto thee, Jerusalem!
O divided house,
Thou shalt crumble to dust,
And swine shall root
Where thy Temple stood!
Woe unto us!

CROWD--(*in a great echoing cry*) Woe unto us!

CENTURION--(*gruffly to hide his embarrassment at being awed by
Lazarus*) Here, you! Drag your carcasses away! (*From each side men

25

Lazarus Laughed

and women come forward to identify and mourn their dead. The wail of lamentation rises and falls. The Centurion looks up at Lazarus-- harshly) You, there! Are you he whom they call the Laugher?

LAZARUS--*(without looking at him--his voice seeming to come from some dream within him)* I am Lazarus.

CENTURION--Who was brought back from death by enchantment?

LAZARUS--*(looking down at him now--with a smile, simply)* No. There is no death!

CHORUS OF FOLLOWERS--*(chanting joyously)* There is no death!

FOLLOWERS--*(echoing)* There is no death!

AN ORTHODOX MAN--*(bending beside the body of Lazarus' Father)* Here is your father, Lazarus. He is dead.

AN ORTHODOX WOMAN--This is your mother, Lazarus. She is dead.

A NAZARENE--Here is your sister, Martha, Lazarus. She is dead.

A NAZARENE WOMAN--And this is Mary, Lazarus. She is dead.

MIRIAM--*(suddenly--with deep grief)* And Jesus who was the Son of Man, who loved you and gave you life again has died, Lazarus--has died!

LAZARUS--*(in a great triumphant voice)* Yes! Yes!! Yes!!! Men die! Even a Son of Man must die to show men that Man may live! But there is no death!

CENTURION--*(at first in a tone of great awe--to his Soldiers)* Is he a god? *(then gruffly, ashamed of his question)* Come down, Jew! I have orders to bring you to Rome to Cæsar!

LAZARUS--*(as if he were answering not the Centurion but the command of his fate from the sky)* Yes! *(He walks down the narrow stairs and, Miriam following him, comes down the path to the road. He goes and kneels for a moment each beside the bodies of his Father, Mother, and Sisters and kisses each in turn on the forehead. For a moment the struggle with his grief can be seen in his face. Then he looks up to the stars and, as if answering a question, again says simply and accept-ingly)* Yes! *(then exultantly)* Yes!! *(And begins to laugh from the depths of his exalted spirit. The laughter of his Chorus and then of his Followers echoes his. The music and dancing begin again.*

(*The Centurion grins sheepishly. The Soldiers chuckle. The Centurion laughs awkwardly. The Soldiers laugh. The music from the house and the laughter of the Followers grow louder. The infection spreads to the Chorus of Old Men whose swaying grief falls into the rhythm of the laughter and music as does that of the mourners.*)

LAZARUS' FOLLOWERS--(*led by their Chorus*) Laugh! Laugh!

CHORUS OF OLD MEN--(*torn by the conflict--torturedly*)

Ha-ha-ha--
Woe to us, woe!

CROWD--(*beside the bodies*)

Woe to us, woe!
Ha-ha--!

CENTURION--(*laughingly*) You are brave, you Laugher! Remember Tiberius never laughs! And boast not to Cæsar there is no death, or he will invent a new one for you!

LAZARUS--(*with a smile*) But all death is men's invention! So laugh! (*He laughs and the Centurion and Soldiers laugh with him, half dancing clumsily now to the beat of the music.*)

CHORUS OF LAZARUS' FOLLOWERS--

Laugh! Laugh!
Fear is no more!
There is no death!
There is only life!
There is only laughter!

FOLLOWERS--(*dancing*)

Laugh! Laugh!
Fear is no more!
Death is dead!

CHORUS OF OLD MEN--(*forgetting their grief--their eyes on Lazarus now, their arms outstretched to him as are those of the crowd grouped around the bodies but forgetting them*)

27

Lazarus Laughed

Death is no more!
Death is dead!
Laugh!

CROWD--

Laugh! Laugh!
Death is no more!

CENTURION--(*laughing, to his laughing Soldiers*) Forward! (*They tramp, dancing, off. Lazarus and Miriam start to follow.*)

MIRIAM--(*suddenly pointing to his Followers who are dancing and laughing obliviously--pityingly*) But your faithful ones who love you, Lazarus?

LAZARUS--(*simply, with a trace of a sad sternness*) This is their test. Their love must remember--or it must forget. Come! (*With a last gesture back like a blessing on all he is leaving, he goes. The laughter of the Soldiers recedes. That of the Chorus of Old Men and of the Crowd falters and breaks into lamenting grief again, guilt-stricken because of its laughter.*)

CHORUS OF OLD MEN--

Laugh! Laugh!
Death is dead!
Laugh!--But woe!
There lie our dead!
Oh shame and guilt!
We forget our dead!

CROWD--(*with fierce remorseful grief*)

Woe to us, woe!
There lie our dead!

CHORUS OF LAZARUS' FOLLOWERS--(*their voices and the music growing more and more hesitating and faint*)

Laugh! Laugh!
There is only life!
There is only--
Laugh--

(*Their dance is faltering and slow now.*)

Fear is no--
Death is--
Laugh--

(The music and dancing and voices cease. The lights in the windows, which have been growing dim, go out. There is a second of complete, death-like silence. The mourning folk in the foreground are frozen figures of grief. Then a sudden swelling chorus of forlorn bewilderment, a cry of lost children comes from the Chorus of Followers and the Followers themselves. They huddle into groups on the roof and on the terrace. They stretch their arms out in every direction supplicatingly.)

CHORUS OF FOLLOWERS--

Oh, Lazarus, laugh!
Do not forsake us!
We forget!
Where is thy love fled?
Give back thy laughter,
Thy fearless laughter!
We forget!

FOLLOWERS--

Give back thy laughter!
We forget!

CHORUS OF FOLLOWERS--*(with dull, resigned terror now)*

Death slinks out
Of his grave in the heart!
Ghosts of fear
Creep back in the brain!
We remember fear!
We remember death!

FOLLOWERS--

Death in the heart!
Fear in the brain!
We remember fear!
We remember death!

CHORUS OF FOLLOWERS--*(wailing hopelessly now)*

Lazarus Laughed

Forgotten is laughter!
We remember
Only death!
Fear is God!
Forgotten is laughter!
Life is death!

FOLLOWERS--

Forgotten is laughter!
Life is death!

ALL--(*the Chorus of Old Men and the Crowd joining in*)

Life is a fearing,
A long dying,
From birth to death!
God is a slayer!
Life is death!

(*Curtain*)

ACT TWO

SCENE ONE

SCENE--*Some months later. A square in Athens about ten o'clock at night. In the rear, pure and beautiful in the light of a full moon, is the façade of a temple. An excited crowd of Greeks of both sexes is gathered in the square as if for some public festival. They are masked according to the scheme of Seven Periods in Seven Types of Character for each sex. Here, of course, the foundation of the mask is the Grecian type of face.*

On the left, the Chorus of Greeks is grouped, seven in number, facing front, in the spearhead formation. As before the Chorus wears masks double the life size of the Crowd masks. They are all of the Proud Self-Reliant type, in the period of Young Manhood.

These seven are clad in goat skins, their tanned bodies and masks daubed and stained with wine lees, in imitation of the old followers of Dionysus. Rumor has led them to hope and believe that Lazarus may be the reincarnation of this deity.

The people in the crowd are holding themselves in restraint with difficulty, they stir and push about restlessly with an eager curiosity and impatience. All eyes are fixed off left.

A buzz of voices hums in the air.

Acting as police, a number of Roman legionaries (masked like the soldiers of Scene Two) armed with staves, keep back the crowd from the line of the street that runs from left to right, front. They resent this duty, which has already kept them there a long time, and are surly and quick-tempered with the Greeks.

Lazarus Laughed

At front, pacing impatiently up and down, is a young Roman noble of twenty-one, clad richly, wearing beautifully wrought armor and helmet. This is Gaius, the heir of Tiberius Cæsar, nicknamed Caligula by the soldiers in whose encampments he was born and where he spent his childhood. His body is bony and angular, almost malformed, with wide, powerful shoulders and long arms and hands, and short, skinny, hairy legs like an ape's. He wears a half-mask of crimson, dark with a purplish tinge, that covers the upper part of his face to below the nose. This mask accentuates his bulging, prematurely wrinkled forehead, his hollow temples and his bulbous, sensual nose. His large troubled eyes, of a glazed greenish-blue, glare out with a shifty feverish suspicion at everyone. Below his mask his own skin is of an anemic transparent pallor. Above it, his hair is the curly blond hair of a child of six or seven. His mouth also is childish, the red lips soft and feminine in outline. Their expression is spoiled, petulant and self-obsessed, weak but domineering. In combination with the rest of the face there is an appalling morbid significance to his mouth. One feels that its boyish cruelty, encouraged as a manly attribute in the coarse brutality of camps, has long ago become naïvely insensitive to any human suffering but its own.

Walking with Caligula is Cneius Crassus, a Roman general--a squat, muscular man of sixty, his mask that of a heavy battered face full of coarse humor.

CHORUS OF GREEKS--(*intoning solemnly*)

Soon the God comes!
Redeemer and Savior!
Dionysus, Son of Man and a God!

GREEK CROWD--(*echoing*)

Soon the God comes
Redeemer and Savior!
Dionysus!

FIRST GREEK--They say an unearthly flame burns in this Lazarus!

SECOND GREEK--The sacred fire! He must be the Fire-born, the son of Zeus!

THIRD GREEK--Many who have seen him swear he is Dionysus, rearisen from Hades!

FOURTH GREEK--(*importantly*) I saw Lazarus at Antioch where the galley on which they were taking him to Rome had been thrice blown back by a storm. Fear of this warning omen is why they now march with him by land.

FIRST GREEK--Does he truly resemble a god?

FOURTH GREEK--(*impressively*) One look in his eyes while his laughter sings in your ears and you forget sorrow! You dance! You laugh! It is as if a heavy weight you had been carrying all your life without knowing it suddenly were lifted. You are like a cloud, you can fly, your mind reels with laughter, you are drunk with joy! (*solemnly*) Take my word for it, he is indeed a god. Everywhere the people have acclaimed him. He heals the sick, he raises the dead, by laughter.

SEVENTH GREEK--But I have heard that when he has gone people cannot remember his laughter, that the dead are dead again and the sick die, and the sad grow more sorrowful.

FIFTH GREEK--Well, we shall soon see with our own eyes. But why should the God return in the body of a Jew?

SIXTH GREEK--What better disguise if he wishes to remain un-known? The fools of Romans will never suspect him!

THIRD GREEK--(*laughing*) Never! They are beginning to claim he is a Roman!

FIFTH GREEK--So much the better! He will be in their confidence!

FOURTH GREEK--He will lead us against Rome! He will laugh our tyrants into the sea! Ha! (*He turns toward the Romans and laughs sneeringly. This is taken up by the Crowd--unpleasant, resentful laughter. They push forward aggressively and almost sweep the Sol-diers from their feet.*)

CRASSUS--(*angrily*) Drive them back!

CALIGULA--(*suddenly with a distorted warped smile*) Order them to use their swords, Cneius. Let the scum look at their dead and learn respect for us!

SOLDIERS--(*shoving and whacking*) Back! Step back! Back there! (*The Crowd push back to their former line. There are muttered curses, groans, protests, which subside into the former hum of expectancy.*)

CALIGULA--(*with the same smile*) The sword, my old hyena! Corpses are so educational!

CRASSUS--(*surlily*) I would like to, I promise you! When I see how they hate us--!

CALIGULA--(*carelessly*) Let them hate--so long as they fear us! We must keep death dangling (*he makes the gesture of doing so*) before their eyes! (*He gives a soft, cruel laugh.*) Will you not sacrifice in my honor? What are a few Greeks? (*queerly*) I like to watch men die.

CRASSUS--I dare not, Caligula. Cæsar has forbidden bloodshed.

CALIGULA--Tiberius is a miser. He wants to hoard all of death for his own pleasure! (*He laughs again.*)

CRASSUS--(*with rough familiarity*) I wager no one will make that complaint against you when you are Cæsar! (*He chuckles.*)

CALIGULA--(*with the sudden grandiose posturing of a bad actor unintentionally burlesquing grandeur*) When I, Gaius Caligula, am Cæsar, I--(*then superstitiously looking up at the sky with cringing foreboding*) But it brings bad luck to anticipate fate. (*He takes off his helmet and spits in it--then with a grim smile*) The heirs of a Cæsar take sick so mysteriously! Even with you who used to ride me on your knee, I do not eat nor drink until you have tasted first.

CRASSUS--(*nodding approvingly*) You are sensible. I suppose I, too, have my price--if they were only clever enough to discover it! (*He laughs hoarsely.*)

CALIGULA--(*steps back from him with an uneasy shudder*) You are honest, at least--too honest, Cneius! (*grimly*) If my father Germanicus had had you for his counselor, he might have escaped their poison. (*then gloomily*) I must fear everyone. The world is my enemy.

CRASSUS--Kill it then! (*He laughs again.*)

CHORUS--(*stretching out their arms in the direction from which Lazarus is expected--supplicatingly*)

Son of the Lightning!
Deadly thy vengeance!
Swift thy deliverance!
Beholding thy Mother,
Greece, our Mother,
Her beauty in bondage,
Her pride in chains!
Hasten, Redeemer!

CROWD--(*as before--echoing the chant*)

Hasten, Redeemer!
Son of the Lightning!
Deadly thy vengeance!
Swift thy deliverance!

CALIGULA--(*disdainfully*) What clods! Mob is the same everywhere, eager to worship any new charlatan! They have already convinced themselves this Lazarus is a reincarnation of Dionysus! A Jew become a god! By the breasts of Venus that *is* a miracle! (*He laughs.*)

CRASSUS--(*seriously*) But he must be expert in magic. He was buried four days and came out unharmed. Maybe he is not a Jew. Some say his father was really a legionary of our garrison in Judea. And he teaches people to laugh at death. That smacks of Roman blood!

CALIGULA--(*ironically*) Better still! He tells them there is no death at all! Hence the multitude of fools who have acclaimed him everywhere since he left his own country--and why Tiberius has begun to fear his influence.

CRASSUS--(*sententiously*) Whom Cæsar fears--disappears!

CALIGULA--Yes, the dupes who follow Lazarus will be killed. But Tiberius believes this Lazarus may know a cure for death or for renewing youth, and the old lecher hopes he can worm the secret out of him--before he kills him. (*He laughs ironically, then disgustedly*) That is why I must escort this Jew to Rome--as a special honor! (*with fierce, haughty resentment*) I, the heir of Cæsar! (*savagely*) Oh, if I were Cæsar--!

CRASSUS--(*with a coarse, meaning smirk*) Patience. Tiberius is old.

CALIGULA--(*suddenly becoming terribly uneasy at some thought*) Cneius! What if this Lazarus has really discovered a cure for old age and should reveal it to Tiberius! (*His lips tremble, his eyes are terrified, he shrinks against Crassus for protection--with boyish pleading*) Oh, Cneius, what could I do then?

CRASSUS--(*matter-of-factly*) Kill him before Cæsar can talk to him.

CALIGULA--(*almost in tears*) But if he knows a charm against death how could he be slain, old fool?

CRASSUS--(*gruffly*) Bah! (*then with grim humor*) Death in bed I suspect, but when men are killed I know they stay dead! (*disgustedly*) A moment ago you were laughing at him! (*scornfully*) Do you fear him now?

CALIGULA--(*rather shamefacedly pulls himself together--then broodingly*) I fear everyone who lives. Even you. As you advised me. (*He turns away.*)

CRASSUS--(*contemptuously*) Well, maybe he can teach you to laugh at fear. You would welcome him then, eh, cry baby?

CALIGULA--(*with sudden passionate intensity but only half aloud as if to himself*) I would love him, Cneius! As a father! As a god! (*He stands staring before him strangely. There is a new stir from the Crowd who again push forward.*)

CRASSUS--(*pointing off right*) Look! I see a great crowd! Your Lazarus must be coming at last!

CHORUS--(*chanting in a deep, rhythmic monotone like the rising and falling cadences of waves on a beach*)

He comes, the Redeemer and Savior!
Laughing along the mountains!
To give back our lost laughter
To raise from the dead our freedom
To free us from Rome!

CROWD--(*echoing this chant*)

Fire-born! Redeemer! Savior!
Raise from the dead our freedom!
Give back our lost laughter!
Free us from Rome!

(*They have been pushing forward, more and more fiercely and defiantly. The Roman Soldiers in spite of their efforts are pushed backward step by step.*)

SOLDIERS--(*angrily*) Back! Back! (*The Soldiers work with a will, dealing out blows with their staves at everyone in reach. But now these blows seem only to infuriate the Crowd which steadily pushes them back into the street. At the same time the distant sound of exultant music, singing and laughter becomes steadily louder. Both Soldiers and Crowd are inspired to battle by these strains without their knowing it. Caligula is listening spell-bound, his mouth open, his body swaying and twitching. Even Crassus stares off at the oncomers, forgetful of the growing plight of his Soldiers.*)

CROWD--(*led by their Chorus--angrily*)

Cowards! Pigs!
Strike! Hit!
Stones! Knives!
Stab! Kill!
Death to the Romans!
Death!

A SOLDIER--(*alarmed, calls to Crassus*) General! Let us use our swords!

SOLDIERS--(*enraged--eagerly*) Yes! Swords!

CROWD--Death!

CRASSUS--(*turning--uneasy but afraid to give any drastic order*) Bah! Staves are enough. Crack their skulls!

CROWD--(*led by the Chorus--defiantly*)

Death to Crassus!
Drunkard! Coward!
Death to him!

(*They continue to push forward, hooting and jeering.*)

CRASSUS--(*exploding for a second*) By the gods--! (*to the Soldiers*) Draw your swords! (*The troops do so eagerly. The Crowd sag back momentarily with exclamations of fear.*)

Lazarus Laughed

CALIGULA--(*listening as in a trance to the music and what is going on behind him--in a queer whisper*) Kill, Cneius! Let me dance! Let me sing! (*The music and crashing of cymbals and the ferment of passions around him cause him to lose all control over himself. He gives a crazy leap in the air and begins to dance grotesquely and chant in a thick voice.*) He is coming! Death, the Deliverer! Kill, soldiers! I command you! I, Caligula! I will be Cæsar! Death!

CROWD--(*led by the Chorus--savage now*)

Beast! Cur!
Death to Caligula!

(*They crowd forward.*)

CALIGULA--(*drawing his sword and flourishing it drunkenly--his eyes glazed*) Death!

CRASSUS--(*drawing his own sword in a frenzy*) Strike! Death! (*His Soldiers raise their swords. The Crowd have raised whatever weapons they have found--knives, clubs, daggers, stones, bare fists.*)

CHORUS--(*chanting fiercely*) Death!

ALL--(*Romans and Greeks alike as one great voice*) Death! (*The chorused word beats down all sound into a stricken silence. The wild joyous music ceases. The Romans and Greeks seem to lean back from one another and collect strength to leap forward. At this moment the voice of Lazarus comes ringing through the air like a command from the sky.*)

LAZARUS--There is no death! (*The Soldiers and Greeks remain frozen in their attitudes of murderous hate. Following his words the laughter of Lazarus is heard, exultant and gaily mocking, filling them with the sheepish shame of children caught in mischief. Their hands hang, their arms sink to their sides. The music starts once more with a triumphant dash of cymbals, Lazarus' laughter is echoed from the throats of the multitude of his Followers who now come dancing into the square, preceded by a band of masked musicians and by their Chorus.*)

(*This Chorus wears, in double size, the laughing mask of Lazarus' Followers in the same Period and Type as in the preceding scene, except that here the mask of each member of the Chorus has a different racial basis--Egyptian, Syrian, Cappadocian, Lydian, Phrygian, Cilician,*)

38

Parthian. The Followers are costumed and masked as in the preceding scene, seven Types in seven Periods, except that, as in the Chorus, racially there are many nations represented. All have wreaths of ivy in their hair and flowers in their hands which they scatter about. They whirl in between the Soldiers and Crowd, forcing them back from each other, teasing them, sifting into the Crowd, their Chorus in a half circle, confronting the Chorus of Greeks.)

CHORUS OF FOLLOWERS--

Laugh! Laugh!
There is no death!
There is only life!
There is only laughter!

FOLLOWERS--(*echoing*)

Laugh! Laugh!
There is no death!

(*Caligula and Crassus are swept to one side, left. Then the cries and laughter of all become mingled into one exclamation.*)

ALL--Lazarus! Lazarus! (*The squad of Roman Soldiers led by the Centurion, who had taken Lazarus prisoner, march in with dancers' steps, like a proud guard of honor now, laughing, pulling a chariot in which Lazarus stands dressed in a tunic of white and gold, his bronzed face and limbs radiant in the halo of his own glowing light.*)

(*Lazarus now looks less than thirty-five. His countenance now might well be that of the positive masculine Dionysus, closest to the soil of the Grecian Gods, a Son of Man, born of a mortal. Not the coarse, drunken Dionysus, nor the effeminate God, but Dionysus in his middle period, more comprehensive in his symbolism, the soul of the recurring seasons, of living and dying as processes in eternal growth, of the wine of life stirring forever in the sap and blood and loam of things. Miriam is beside him, dressed in black, smiling the same sad tender smile, holding Lazarus' arm as if for protection and in protection. She appears older, a woman over forty-five.*)

CHORUS OF GREEKS--(*rushing to Lazarus' car*)

Hail, Dionysus!
Iacchus!

Lazarus Laughed

Lazarus!
Hail!

(*They surround him, throw over his shoulders and head the finely dressed hide of a bull with great gilded horns, force into his right hand the mystic rod of Dionysus with a pine cone on top, then prostrate themselves.*)

Hail, Savior!
Redeemer!
Conqueror of Death!

ALL--(*in a repeated chorus which finally includes even the Roman Soldiers, raising their arms to him*)

Hail, Lazarus!
Redeemer!
Hail!

(*They are silent. Lazarus looks at them, seeming to see each and all at the same time, and his laughter, as if in answer to their greetings, is heard rising from his lips like a song.*)

CRASSUS--(*awed*) Look! He is more than man!

CALIGULA--(*trembling, in a queer agitation*) I dare not look!

CRASSUS--Do you hear his laughter?

CALIGULA--(*chokingly--puts his hands over his ears*) I will not hear!

CRASSUS--But you must welcome him in Cæsar's name!

CALIGULA--(*his teeth chattering*) I must kill him!

LAZARUS--(*looking directly at him--gaily mocking*) Death is dead, Caligula! (*He begins to laugh again softly.*)

CALIGULA--(*with an hysterical cry of defiant terror*) You lie! (*Sword in hand he whirls to confront Lazarus, but at the first sight of his face he stops in his tracks, trembling, held fascinated by Lazarus' eyes, mumbling with a last pitiful remainder of defiance*) But--you lie-- whatever you are! I say there *must* be death! (*The sword has fallen to his side. He stares open-mouthed at Lazarus. There is something of a shy, wondering child about his attitude now. Lazarus looks at him, laughing with gentle understanding. Caligula suddenly drops his*

40

sword and covering his face with his hands weeps like a boy who has been hurt.) You have murdered my only friend, Lazarus! Death would have been my slave when I am Cæsar. He would have been my jester and made me laugh at fear! (*He weeps bitterly.*)

LAZARUS--(*gaily*) Be your own jester instead, O Caligula! Laugh at yourself, O Cæsar-to-be! (*He laughs. The Crowd now all join in with him.*

(*Caligula suddenly uncovers his face, grins his warped grin, gives a harsh cackle which cracks through the other laughter with a splitting discord, cuts a hopping caper like some grotesque cripple which takes him to the side of Lazarus' chariot where he squats on his hams and, stretching out his hand, fingers Lazarus' robe inquisitively and stares up into his face in the attitude of a chained monkey.*)

CALIGULA--(*with a childish, mischievous curiosity*) Then if there is no death, O Teacher, tell me why I love to kill?

LAZARUS--Because you fear to die! (*then gaily mocking*) But what do you matter, O Deathly-Important One? Put yourself that question-- as a jester! (*exultantly*) Are you a speck of dust danced in the wind? Then laugh, dancing! Laugh yes to your insignificance! Thereby will be born your new greatness! As Man, Petty Tyrant of Earth, you are a bubble pricked by death into a void and a mocking silence! But as dust, you are eternal change, and everlasting growth, and a high note of laughter soaring through chaos from the deep heart of God! Be proud, O Dust! Then you may love the stars as equals! (*then mockingly again*) And then perhaps you may be brave enough to love even your fellow men without fear of their vengeance!

CALIGULA--(*dully*) I cannot understand. I hate men. I am afraid of their poison and their swords and the cringing envy in their eyes that only yields to fear!

LAZARUS--(*gaily mocking*) Tragic is the plight of the tragedian whose only audience is himself! Life is for each man a solitary cell whose walls are mirrors. Terrified is Caligula by the faces he makes! But I tell you to laugh in the mirror, that seeing your life gay, you may begin to live as a guest, and not as a condemned one! (*raising his hands for silence--with a playful smile*) Listen! In the dark peace of the grave the man called Lazarus rested. He was still weak, as one who recovers from a long illness--for, living, he had believed his life a sad

41

one! (*He laughs softly, and softly they all echo his laughter.*) He lay dreaming to the croon of silence, feeling as the flow of blood in his own veins the past reenter the heart of God to be renewed by faith into the future. He thought: "Men call this death"--for he had been dead only a little while and he still remembered. Then, of a sudden, a strange gay laughter trembled from his heart as though his life, so long repressed in him by fear, had found at last its voice and a song for singing. "Men call this death," it sang. "Men call life death and fear it. They hide from it in horror. Their lives are spent in hiding. Their fear becomes their living. They worship life as death!"

CHORUS OF FOLLOWERS--(*in a chanting echo*)

Men call life death and fear it.
They hide from it in horror.
Their lives are spent in hiding.
Their fear becomes their living.
They worship life as death!

LAZARUS--And here the song of Lazarus' life grew pitiful. "Men must learn to live," it mourned. "Before their fear invented death they knew, but now they have forgotten. They must be taught to laugh again!" And Lazarus answered "Yes!" (*He now addresses the Crowd--especially Caligula, directly, laughingly.*) Thus sang his life to Lazarus while he lay dead! Man must learn to live by laughter! (*He laughs.*)

CHORUS OF FOLLOWERS--

Laugh! Laugh!
There is only life!
There is only laughter!
Fear is no more!
Death is dead!

CHORUS OF GREEKS--

Laugh! Laugh!
Hail, Dionysus!
Fear is no more!
Thou hast conquered death!

42

ALL--(*laughing--in a great laughing chorus*)

Laugh! Laugh!
Fear is no more!
Death is dead!

LAZARUS--(*as to a crowd of children--laughingly*) Out with you! Out into the woods! Upon the hills! Cities are prisons wherein man locks himself from life. Out with you under the sky! Are the stars too pure for your sick passions? Is the warm earth smelling of night too desirous of love for your pale introspective lusts? Out! Let laughter be your new clean lust and sanity! So far man has only learned to snicker meanly at his neighbor! Let a laughing away of self be your new right to live forever! Cry in your pride, "I am Laughter, which is Life, which is the Child of God!" (*He laughs and again his voice leads and dominates the rhythmic chorus of theirs. The music and dancing begin again.*)

THE TWO CHORUSES--(*chanting in unison*)

Laugh! Laugh!
There is only God!
We are His Laughter!

ALL--(*echoing*)

There is only God!
We are His Laughter!
Laugh! Laugh!

(*They take hold of his chariot traces, and as he had come, in the midst of a happy multitude, now augmented by all the Greeks, and the Roman Soldiers who had awaited him, dancing, playing, singing, laughing, he is escorted off. The noise of their passing recedes. Caligula and Crassus are left in the empty square, the former squatting on his hams, monkey-wise, and brooding somberly.*)

CRASSUS--(*is swaying and staggering, like a man in a drunken stupor, in a bewildered, stubborn struggle to control himself. He stammers after the Soldiers*) Ha-ha-ha--Halt! Halt, I say! No use--they are gone--mutiny--Halt! (*He continues to stumble toward left.*) Ha-ha-- Stop it, curse you! Am I laughing? Where am I going? After Lazarus? Thirty years of discipline and I--Halt, traitor! Remember Cæsar! Remember Rome! Halt, traitor! (*He faints with the violence of his struggle and falls in a limp heap.*)

CALIGULA--(*startled by his fall, terrified, hops to his feet and snatches up his sword defensively, glancing over his shoulder and whirling around as if he expected someone to stab him in the back. Then, forcing a twisted grin of self-contempt--harshly*) Coward! What do I fear--if there is no death? (*As if he had to cut something, he snatches up a handful of flowers--desperately*) You must laugh, Caligula! (*He starts to lop off the flowers from their stems with a savage intentness.*) Laugh! Laugh! Laugh! (*Finally, impatiently, he cuts off all the remaining with one stroke.*) Laugh! (*He grinds the petals under his feet and breaks out into a terrible hysterical giggle.*) Ha-ha--

(*Curtain*)

SCENE TWO

SCENE--*A midnight, months later. Immediately inside the walls of Rome. In the foreground is the portico of a temple between whose massive columns one looks across a street on a lower level to the high wall of Rome at the extreme rear. In the center of the wall is a great metal gate. The night is thick and oppressive. In the sky overhead lightning flashes and thunder rumbles and crashes but there is no rain.*

Within the portico on rows of chairs placed on a series of wide steps which are on each side, members of the Senate are seated in their white robes. High hanging lamps cast a wan light over their faces. They are all masked in the Roman mask, refined in them by nobility of blood but at the same time with strength degenerated, corrupted by tyranny and debauchery to an exhausted cynicism. The three periods of Middle Age, Maturity and Old Age are represented in the types of the Self-Tortured, Introspective; Proud, Self-Reliant; the Servile, Hypocritical; the Cruel, Revengeful; and the Resigned, Sorrowful. The Senators are divided into two groups on each side, thirty in each. Seated in the middle of the lower of the three high broad stairs that lead to the level from which the columns rise is the Chorus of Senators, seven in number, facing front, in double-sized masks of the Servile, Hypocritical type of Old Age.

Lazarus, in his robe of white and gold, the aura of light surrounding his body seeming to glow more brightly than ever, stands in the rear at the edge of the portico, center, gazing upward into the pall of sky beyond the wall. His figure appears in its immobility to be the statue of the god of the temple. Near him, but to the rear and to the left of him, facing right, Miriam is kneeling in her black robes, swaying backward and forward, praying silently with moving lips like a nun who asks mercy for the sins of the world. She has grown much older, her hair is gray, her shoulders are bowed.

On the other side, placed similarly in relation to Lazarus and facing Miriam, Caligula is squatting on his hams on a sort of throne-chair of

Lazarus Laughed

ivory and gold. He is dressed with foppish richness in extreme bright colors, a victory wreath around his head. He stares blinkingly and inquisitively at Lazarus, then at Miriam. He is half-drunk. A large figured goblet of gold is in his hand. A slave with an amphora of wine crouches on the steps by his chair. The slave wears a black negroid mask.

At the opening of the scene there is heard the steady tramp of departing troops, whose masks, helmets and armored shoulders can be seen as they pass through the street before Lazarus to the gate beyond. Finally with a metallic clash the gate is shut behind them and there is a heavy and oppressive silence in which only the murmured prayers of Miriam are heard.

CHORUS OF THE SENATE--(*intones wearily, as if under a boring compulsion*)

The Roman Senate
Is the Roman Senate
The Mighty Voice
Of the Roman People
As long as Rome is Rome.

CALIGULA--(*as if he hadn't heard--sings hoarsely an old camp song of the Punic Wars, pounding with his goblet*)

A bold legionary am I!
March, oh march on!
A Roman eagle was my daddy,
My mother was a drunken drabby
Oh, march on to the wars!

Since lived that lady Leda
March, oh march on!
Women have loved high-fliers
And we are eagles of Rome!
Oh march on to the wars!

Comrades, march to the wars!
There's pretty girls in Carthage
And wine to swill in Carthage,

46

So we must capture Carthage
And fight for Mother Rome!

(*Holds out his goblet to be refilled. There is silence again. He stares at Lazarus with a somber intentness. He says thickly*) The legions have gone, Lazarus. (*Lazarus gives no evidence of having heard him. Caligula gulps at his wine. The Senators begin to talk to each other in low voices.*)

FIRST SENATOR--How does that Jew make that light come from him, I wonder? It is a well-contrived bit of magic.

SECOND SENATOR--What are we waiting for? A messenger came to me with Cæsar's command that the Senate meet here at midnight.

THIRD SENATOR--(*bored*) Some new whim of Tiberius, naturally--(*with a meaning titter*)--or rather I should say, unnaturally!

FOURTH SENATOR--Perhaps Cæsar has decided to abolish our august body by a massacre in mass!

THIRD SENATOR--(*yawning*) There was a feast at Cinna's last night that lasted until this evening. I could welcome my own murder as an excuse for sleeping!

FIFTH SENATOR--(*pompously*) Tiberius would not dare harm the Senate. He may mistreat individual Senators, but the Roman Senate is the Roman Senate!

CHORUS OF THE SENATE--(*as before--wearily as if under a boring compulsion--intones*)

While Rome is Rome
The Senate is the Senate
The Mighty Voice of the Roman People.

FIRST SENATOR--(*with the ghost of a laugh--wearily*) The Senate is an empty name--a pack of degenerate cowards with no trace of their ancient nobility or courage remaining--that and no more!

THIRD SENATOR--(*flippantly*) You are too severe with yourself, Lucius! (*a titter of laughter*)

FIRST SENATOR--(*wearily*) A degenerate coward. I am, I confess it. So are you too, Sulpicius--a hundred fold!--whether you admit it or not. (*Sulpicius laughs weakly without taking offense.*)

SIXTH SENATOR--(*after a pause--sighing*) In truth, the Senate is not what it used to be. I can remember--

FIRST SENATOR--Let us forget, if we can! (*then impatiently*) What are we doing here?

SECOND SENATOR--I imagine it has something to do with the followers of this Lazarus encamped outside the wall. Probably the legions are to butcher them in their sleep.

SEVENTH SENATOR--And what part do we play--official witnesses? But how can we witness at night and through a wall? (*with bored resignation*) Ah well, the moods of Tiberius are strange, to say the least. But Cæsar is Cæsar.

CHORUS--(*again with bored weariness as before*)

Hail!
Cæsar is Cæsar
The August One
Prince of the Senate
Tribune over Tribunes
Consul of Consuls
Supreme Pontiff
Emperor of Rome
God among Gods
Hail!

FIRST SENATOR--(*after a pause of silence--dryly*) Cæsar is a beast--and a madman!

FIFTH SENATOR--(*pompously*) Respect, sir! More respect for Cæsar!

THIRD SENATOR--(*mockingly*) Or caution, Lucius. One of us might repeat your opinion to him.

FIRST SENATOR--You would if it would pay you. But all my money is squandered. My death is worthless to Tiberius. He would not reward you. Moreover, you would not be revenged on me, for I long for death.

THIRD SENATOR--(*dryly*) Your stomach must be out of order.

FIRST SENATOR--The times are out of order. But let us change the subject. Is it true Tiberius has fled to Capri?

FOURTH SENATOR--Yes. He was terrified by the multitude of laughing idiots who appeared today with that charlatan. (*He points to Lazarus.*)

SECOND SENATOR--There are thousands of them outside the wall. Cæsar refused to let them enter the city. The story is, this Lazarus was dead four days and then restored himself to life by magic.

FIRST SENATOR--I have a mind to question him. (*calls as to a slave*) You, there! Jew, turn round! In the name of the Senate! (*Lazarus seems not to hear him. Lucius remarks with a weary smile*) So much for our authority!

SIXTH SENATOR--(*with injured dignity*) What insolence! (*in a rage*) Ho, barbarian cur, turn round! The Senate commands you! (*Lazarus does not seem to hear, but Caligula turns on them fiercely.*)

CALIGULA--Silence! Leave him alone! (*with insulting scorn*) I, Caligula, command *you*! (*The Senators seem to shrink back from him in fear, all but Lucius, who answers with a mocking servility.*)

FIRST SENATOR--At least, grant us the boon to see this corpse's face, O Gracious Gaius!

CALIGULA--(*fixing his cruel, burning eyes on him--softly*) I heard you wish for death, Lucius. When I am Cæsar you shall scream and pray for it!

FIRST SENATOR--(*dryly and haughtily*) You were bred in camp, Gaius. You should have learned more courage there along with your coarseness. But accept my gratitude for your warning. I shall take care to die before you become Cæsar--and life becomes too idiotic!

CALIGULA--(*his grin becoming ferocious with cruelty*) No. You are too weak to kill yourself. Look at me, Lucius! I am imagining what I shall have done to you! (*The Senators are now trembling. Even Lucius cannot repress a shudder of horror at the face glaring at him. Suddenly Caligula throws the cup from him and springs to his feet.*) What good is wine if it cannot kill thought? Lazarus! It is time. I must give the signal! The legions are waiting. It is Cæsar's command that they spare none of your followers. (*He has walked toward Lazarus.*)

MIRIAM--(*stretches out her hands to Caligula imploringly*) Mercy! Spare them who are so full of life and joy!

49

CALIGULA--(*harshly*) For their joy I will revenge myself upon them! Mercy? If there is no death, then death is a mercy! Ask that man! (*He points accusingly to Lazarus.*) And why should you plead for them, Jewess? There are few Jews among them. They are mostly those whom your people call idolaters and would gladly see murdered.

MIRIAM--(*with deep grief*) I am a mother of dead children. I plead for the mothers of those about to die.

CALIGULA--(*contemptuously*) Pah! (*He turns from her and puts his hand on Lazarus' shoulder.*) Lazarus! Do you hear? I must signal to the legions!

LAZARUS--(*turns. He has grown more youthful. He seems no more than thirty. His face is exalted and calm and beautiful. His eyes shine with an unearthly glory. The Senators lean forward in their seats, fascinated by his face. A low murmur of admiration comes from them. Lazarus speaks commandingly.*) Wait! I will awaken my beloved ones that their passing may be a symbol to the world that there is no death! (*He turns, throwing back his head and stretching up his arms, and begins to laugh low and tenderly, like caressing music at first but gradually gaining in volume, becoming more and more intense and insistent, finally ending up on a triumphant, blood-stirring call to that ultimate attainment in which all prepossession with self is lost in an ecstatic affirmation of Life. The voices of his Followers from beyond the wall, at first one by one, then several at a time, then multitudes, join in his laughter. Even the Senators are drawn into it. Now every one of these is standing up, stretching out his arms toward Lazarus, laughing harshly and discordantly and awkwardly in his attempt to laugh. Terrific flashes of lightning and crashes of thunder seem a responsive accompaniment from the heavens to this laughter of thousands which throbs in beating waves of sound in the air. Mingled with the laughing from beyond the wall comes the sound of singing and the music of flutes and cymbals. Miriam has crawled on her knees to the edge of the portico where her black figure of grief is outlined below and to the left of Lazarus, her arms raised outward like the arms of a cross.*)

FOLLOWERS OF LAZARUS--(*in a great chanting singing chorus*)

Laugh! Laugh!
There is only God!
Life is His Laughter!

We are His Laughter!
Fear is no more!
Death is dead!

CHORUS OF SENATORS--(*taking it up in a tone between chanting and their old solemn intoning*)

Laugh! Laugh!
Fear is no more!
Death is dead!

ALL--(*the multitude beyond the wall, all the Senators, everyone except the never-laughing Miriam and Caligula and the Men of the Legions*)

Laugh! Laugh!
Death is dead!

CALIGULA--(*in a queer state of mingled exaltation and fear-- hopping restlessly about from foot to foot--shouting*) The signal! Shall I give the signal to kill, Lazarus?

MEN OF THE LEGIONS--(*following a brazen trumpet call, are suddenly heard from beyond the wall beginning to laugh their hoarse, bass laughter, a deeper note than all the others*) Laugh! Laugh!

CALIGULA--(*listening--with dismay*) I hear the legions, Lazarus! They are laughing with them! (*He cries with a strange pitifulness and beseeching*) You are playing me false, Lazarus! You are trying to evade death! You are trying to spare your people! You are small and weak like other men when the test comes! You give way to pity! Your great laughter becomes pitiful! (*working himself into a rage*) You are a traitor, Lazarus! You betray Cæsar! Have you forgotten I will be Cæsar? You betray me, Lazarus! (*He rushes to the edge and, making a megaphone of his hands, bellows*) You on the wall! Sentry! It is I, Caligula! Kill! (*The brazen trumpets of the Legions sound from beyond the wall. He springs near Lazarus again, in a fiendish ecstasy, dancing a hopping grotesque sword dance behind him, chanting as he does so*) Kill! Kill laughter! Kill those who deny Cæsar! I will be Cæsar! Kill those who deny Death! I will be Death! My face will be bright with blood! My laughing face, Lazarus! Laughing because men fear me! My face of victorious Fear! Look at me! I am laughing, Lazarus! *My* laughter! Laughter of Gods and Cæsars! Ha-ha-ha-ha! (*He laughs, his laughter fanatically cruel and savage, forced from his lips with a desperate, destroying abandon. For a moment, above all the chorus of other sounds, his voice fights to overcome that of Lazarus, whose laughter seems now to have attained the most exultant heights of spiritual affirmation. Then Caligula's breaks into a cry of fear and a sob, and, casting his sword aside, he hides his face in his hands and cries beseechingly)* Forgive me! I love you, Lazarus! Forgive me! (*At this second the blaring trumpets of the Legions are heard approaching and their great bass chorus of marching tramping laughter.*)

MEN OF THE LEGIONS--(*chanting*)

Laugh! Laugh! Laugh!
Fear, no more!
Death, no more!
Death is dead!

(*There is now no sound of the singing or the laughter or music of Lazarus' Followers. Miriam rocks to and fro and raises a low wail of lamentation. The Senators cheer and shout as at a triumph.*)

CHORUS OF SENATORS--(*saluting Lazarus*)

Hail, Victor!
Hail, Divine One!
Thou hast slain fear!
Thou hast slain death!
Hail! Triumph!

SENATORS--

Hail! Hail!
Slayer of Fear!
Slayer of Death!

(*The gate in the wall is clanged open. The returning Legions burst through and gather in a dense mob in the street below Lazarus, who looks down upon them, silent but smiling gently now. They stare at him with admiration. Only a sea of their masks can be seen, their eyes shining exultantly. Crassus, their general, ascends the steps until he stands a little below Lazarus. Their Chorus of Legionaries in double-sized masks climb to the step below Crassus, forming behind him. They are in the Period of Manhood, of the Simple, Ignorant Type. No weapons can be seen--only their masks and helmets and armor gleaming in the lightning flashes and in the flickering light of torches. Their laughter seems to shake the walls and make the pillars of the temple dance.*)

CHORUS OF THE LEGIONS--

Fear, no more!
Death, no more!
Death is dead!

LEGIONARIES--(*echoing*)

Laugh! Laugh! Laugh!
Death is dead!

CRASSUS--(*raising his hand*) Silence! (*They obey. He turns to Lazarus and bows his head, falling on one knee, raising his right arm.*) Hail!

LEGIONARIES--(*as one man--raising their arms*) Hail!

CALIGULA--(*suddenly pushes forward impudently and strikes a grandiose attitude*) I am here, my brave ones! (*There is a roar of mocking laughter from the Legionaries.*)

CRASSUS--(*not unkindly*) Not you, Little Killer! We hail the Great Laugher!

CALIGULA--(*harshly*) Have you killed all his followers?

CRASSUS--No. They died. They did not wait for our attack. They charged upon us, laughing! They tore our swords away from us, laughing, and we laughed with them! They stabbed themselves, dancing as though it were a festival! They died, laughing, in one another's arms! We laughed, too, with joy because it seemed it was not they who died but death itself they killed! (*He stops uncertainly, bowing to Lazarus, awkwardly*) I do not understand this. I am a soldier. But there is a god in it somewhere! For I know they were drunk, and so were we, with a happiness no mortal ever felt on earth before! And death was dead! (*In a sudden outburst as if he were drunk with excitement, he takes off his helmet and waves it.*) Hail, Deliverer! Death is dead! We left our swords with them! What virtue in killing when there is no death? Your foe laughs. The joke is on you. What a fool's game, eh? One can only laugh! Now we want peace to laugh in--to laugh at war! Let Cæsars fight--that is all they are good for--and not much good for that!

CALIGULA--(*frenziedly*) Silence, impious traitor!

CRASSUS--(*smiling drunkenly*) Shut up, yourself, camp-brat! Though you were Cæsar this minute I would laugh at you! Your death is dead!

We will make Lazarus Cæsar! What say you? (*He appeals to the Soldiers.*)

CALIGULA--No!

CHORUS OF THE LEGIONS--(*with laughing intoxication*) Hail, Lazarus Cæsar! Hail!

LEGIONARIES--Lazarus Cæsar, hail!

CRASSUS--(*appealing to Senate*) And you, Senators!

CHORUS OF SENATORS--(*with the same joyous intoxication as the Soldiers*) Hail, Lazarus Cæsar! Hail!

SENATORS--Lazarus Cæsar, hail!

CALIGULA--(*piteously*) No, Lazarus! Say no for my sake!

LAZARUS--(*with gay mockery*) What is--Cæsar? (*He begins to laugh with mockery. All except Caligula and Miriam join in this laughter.*)

CRASSUS--Ha-ha! What is Cæsar? You are right! You deserve better from us. A god? How is that? We will build you a temple, Lazarus, and make you a god!

LAZARUS--(*laughingly*) When men make gods, there is no God! (*He laughs. They all laugh.*)

CRASSUS--(*with puzzled good-nature*) I do not understand. But there is a god in it somewhere--a god of peace--a god of happiness! Perhaps you are already he, eh? Are you? Well, never mind now, remember our offer. Give us your answer tomorrow. Good night to you!

LAZARUS--(*As the Soldiers start to march away behind Crassus, and the Senators turn to retire, he stops them all for a moment with a gesture--with a deep earnestness*) Wait! When you awake tomorrow, try to remember! Remember that death is dead! Remember to laugh!

ALL--(*as if taking an oath with one voice*) We will remember, Lazarus!

CRASSUS--(*making a sign to the regimental musicians jovially*) And we will laugh! Play there! (*The bands crash out. The Legions tramp away.*)

CHORUS OF THE LEGIONS--(*chanting to the music*)

Laugh! Laugh! Laugh!
Cæsar, no more!
War, no more!
Wounds, no more!
Death is dead!
Dead! Dead! Dead!

LEGIONARIES--

Laugh! Laugh! Laugh!
Death is dead!
Dead! Dead! Dead!

CHORUS OF SENATORS--(*following them*)

Cæsar, no more!
Fear, no more!
Death, no more!
Laugh! Laugh! Laugh!

SENATE--(*elated, excited as a crowd of schoolboys going on a vacation. Marching after them.*)

Laugh! Laugh! Laugh!
Death is dead!

(*Lazarus, Miriam and Caligula remain.*)

LAZARUS--(*with a great yearning*) If men would remember! If they could! (*He stares after them compassionately.*)

CALIGULA--(*crouching beside Lazarus. Plucks at his robe humbly.*) You will not laugh at Cæsar, Lazarus, will you--when I am Cæsar? You will not laugh at gods when they make me a god? (*Lazarus does not answer. Caligula forces a cruel vindictive smile.*) I swear you shall not laugh at death when I am Death! Ha-ha--(*He starts to laugh harshly--then suddenly, terrified, slinks away and sidles off at right.*)

MIRIAM--(*from where she kneels bowed with grief--brokenly*) Those who have just died were like your children, Lazarus. They believed in you and loved you.

LAZARUS--And I loved them!

MIRIAM--Then how could you laugh when they were dying?

LAZARUS--(*exultingly*) Did they not laugh? That was their victory and glory! (*with more and more of a passionate, proud exultation*) Eye to eye with the Fear of Death, did they not laugh with scorn? "Death to old Death," they laughed! "Once as squirming specks we crept from the tides of the sea. Now we return to the sea! Once as quivering flecks of rhythm we beat down from the sun. Now we reenter the sun! Cast aside is our pitiable pretense, our immortal egohood, the holy lantern behind which cringed our Fear of the Dark! Flung off is that impudent insult to life's nobility which gibbers: 'I, this Jew, this Roman, this noble or this slave, must survive in my pettiness forever!' Away with such cowardice of spirit! We will to die! We will to change! Laughing we lived with our gift, now with laughter give we back that gift to become again the Essence of the Giver! Dying we laugh with the Infinite. We are the Giver and the Gift! Laughing, we will our own annihilation! Laughing, we give our lives for Life's sake!" (*He laughs up to heaven ecstatically.*) This must Man will as his end and his new beginning! He must conceive and desire his own passing as a mood of eternal laughter and cry with pride, "Take back, O God, and accept in turn a gift from me, my grateful blessing for Your gift--and see, O God, now I am laughing with You! I am Your laughter--and You are mine!" (*He laughs again, his laughter dying lingeringly and tenderly on his lips like a strain of music receding into the silence over still waters.*)

MIRIAM--(*with a sigh--meekly*) I cannot understand, Lazarus. (*sadly*) They were like your children--and they have died. Must you not mourn for them?

LAZARUS--(*gently*) Mourn? When they laughed?

MIRIAM--(*sadly*) They are gone from us. And their mothers weep.

LAZARUS--(*puts his arm around her and raises her to her feet--tenderly*) But God, their Father, laughs! (*He kisses her on the forehead.*)

(*Curtain*)

ACT THREE

SCENE ONE

SCENE--*Some days later--exterior of Tiberius' villa-palace at Capri. It is about two in the morning of a clear black night. In the rear, the walls of the villa, which is built entirely of marble on the brow of a cliff, loom up with a startling clarity against the sky. The rear foreground is a marble terrace at the middle of which is a triumphal arch. On each side, leading up to it, are massive marble columns standing like the mummies of legionaries at attention. In the exact centre of the arch itself a cross is set up on which a full grown male lion has been crucified. A lamp reflecting downward has been fixed at the top of the cross to light up an inscription placed over the lion's head. Below the steps to the terrace, in a line facing front, on each side of the cross, is the Chorus of the Guard in their double masks and gorgeous uniforms and armor. Their masks are the same as the Legionary Chorus of the previous scene.*

The windows of the palace glow crimson-purple with the reflection of many shaded lamps. The sound of music in a strained theme of that joyless abandon which is vice is heard above a confused drunken clamor of voices, punctuated by the high, staccato laughter of women and youths. A squad of the Guard in the same uniforms as the Chorus, masked as all the Roman Soldiers previously, enter from the left, front, climbing up from the beach below. They are commanded by a Centurion, Flavius. His mask is that of a typical young patrician officer. They are followed by Lazarus and Miriam. Caligula walks behind, his drawn sword in his hand. He is in a state of queer conflicting emotion, seeming to be filled with a nervous dread and terror of everything about him, while at the same time perversely excited and elated by his own morbid tension. Lazarus, looking no more than twenty-five, ha-loed in his own mystic light, walks in a deep, detached serenity.

Miriam, in black, her hair almost white now, her figure bowed and feeble, seems more than ever a figure of a sad, resigned mother of the dead. The Soldiers form in line with the columns.

FLAVIUS--(*saluting Caligula--with an awed glance at Lazarus*) I will announce your coming--(*as if in spite of himself he bows awkwardly to Lazarus*)--and that of this man. Cæsar was not expecting you so soon, I think.

CALIGULA--(*forcing a light tone*) Lazarus laughed and the galley slaves forgot their fetters and made their oars fly as if they were bound for the Blessed Isles of Liberty! (*then with an ironic smile*) But you need not tell Tiberius that, good Flavius. Say it was due to my extreme zeal.

FLAVIUS--(*smiles with respectful understanding. Caligula nods in dismissal. Flavius turns to go--apologetically*) You may have to wait. I dare not speak before he questions me. (*Flavius salutes and hastens to the villa, walking under an arm of the cross unconcernedly without an upward glance. As they follow him with their eyes Caligula and Miriam see the lion for the first time. He steps back with a startled exclamation. She gives a cry of horror and covers her eyes with her hands to shut out the sight.*)

LAZARUS--(*immediately puts his arms around her protectingly*) What is it, Beloved? (*She hides her face on his breast, pointing toward the lion with a trembling hand.*)

CALIGULA--(*pointing--curiously now, but with entire callousness*) This lion they have crucified. Are you frightened, Jewess? (*with a cruel laugh*) My grandfather frequently plants whole orchards of such trees, but usually they bear human fruit!

MIRIAM--(*with a shudder*) Monster!

CALIGULA--(*with genuine surprise--turning to her*) Who? Why? (*He approaches the cross and stares at it moodily.*) But why did he have it placed here where he knew you must pass? Tiberius does not go to such pains to frighten women. (*His eyes fasten on the inscription above the lion's head.*) Aha! I see! (*He reads*) "From the East, land of false gods and superstition, this lion was brought to Rome to amuse

Cæsar." (*A silence. Caligula shrugs his shoulders, turning away--lightly*) A lesson for you, Lazarus. An example for other lions--not to roar--or laugh--at Cæsar! (*He gives a harsh laugh.*) Tiberius must be terribly afraid of you. (*then somberly*) You should never have come here. I would have advised you not to--but what are you to me? My duty, if I wish to become Cæsar, is to Cæsar. Besides, you are no fool. Evidently you must desire your own death. Last night *you* might have been Cæsar. The legions were yours.

LAZARUS--(*smiling without bitterness--with a sad comprehension*) But this morning the legions had forgotten. They only remembered--to go out and pick up their swords! They also pillaged the bodies a little, as their right, believing now that they had slain them! (*this last a bit bitterly*)

CALIGULA--(*tauntingly*) The legions did slay them! It was only by some magician's trick you made them think your followers killed themselves.

LAZARUS--(*not answering him--ironically to himself*) It is too soon. Men still need their swords to slash at ghosts in the dark. Men, those haunted heroes! (*He laughs softly.*)

CALIGULA--(*irritably*) What are you laughing at?

LAZARUS--At Lazarus when I find him feeling wronged because men are men! (*He laughs again, softly and musically.*)

CALIGULA--(*again taunting brutally*) You may be in his place soon! (*He points to the lion.*) Will you laugh then? (*Miriam gives a cry of terror.*)

LAZARUS--(*calmly*) Yes. (*then humbly, bowing his head*) I will laugh with the pride of a beggar set upon the throne of Man!

CALIGULA--(*sneeringly*) You boast. (*then as Lazarus does not answer, touching the lion with intentional provoking brutality*) This one from Africa seems almost gone. They do not last as long as men.

LAZARUS--(*walks up the steps to the cross and, stretching to his full height, gently pushes the lion's hair out of its eyes--tenderly*) Poor brother! Cæsar avenges himself on you because of me. Forgive me your suffering!

CALIGULA--(*with a start backward--with frightened awe*) Gods! He licks your hand! I could swear he smiles--with his last breath! (*then with relief*) Now he is dead!

LAZARUS--(*gently*) There is no death.

CALIGULA--(*pointing to the lion*) What is that then?

LAZARUS--Your fear of life.

CALIGULA--(*impatiently*) Bah! (*then somberly*) A little fear is useful even for lions--or teachers of laughter if they wish to laugh long! (*then with a sudden exasperation*) Escape now, you fool, while there is still time!

LAZARUS--(*laughing softly*) Escape--what?

CALIGULA--(*in a frenzy*) You know, you ass, you lunatic! Escape death! Death! Death! (*to Miriam*) You, woman! Talk to him! Do you want him nailed up like that?

MIRIAM--(*with a pitiful cry*) Lazarus! Come! Caligula will help us!

CALIGULA--(*harshly*) You presume, Jewess! I have no wish to die! (*then with his wry smile*) But I will turn my back--and shut my eyes-- (*He walks away to left.*)

MIRIAM--(*beseechingly*) Lazarus! I could not bear that aching hunger of my empty heart if you should die again!

LAZARUS--(*coming to her--tenderly*) I will not leave you! Believe in me! (*He kisses her forehead tenderly.*)

MIRIAM--(*after a pause--slowly and lamentingly*) I wish we were home, Lazarus. This Roman world is full of evil. These skies threaten. These hearts are heavy with hatred. There is a taint of blood in the air that poisons the breath of the sea. These columns and arches and thick walls seem waiting to fall, to crush these rotten men and then to crumble over the bones that raised them until both are dust. It is a world deadly to your joy, Lazarus. Its pleasure is a gorging of dirt, its fulfilled desire a snoring in a sty in the mud among swine. Its will is so sick that it must kill in order to be aware of life at all. I wish we were home, Lazarus. I begin to feel horror gnawing at my breast. I begin to know the torture of the fear of death, Lazarus--not of my death but of yours--not of the passing of your man's body but of the going away from me of your laughter which is to me as my son, my little boy!

LAZARUS--(*soothing her*) Be comforted, Beloved. Your fear shall never be!

MIRIAM--On the hills near Bethany you might pray at noon and laugh your boy's laughter in the sun and there would be echoing laughter from the sky and up from the grass and distantly from the shining sea. We would adopt children whose parents the Romans had butchered, and their laughter would be around me in my home where I cooked and weaved and sang. And in the dawn at your going out, and in the evening on your return, I would hear in the hushed air the bleating of sheep and the tinkling of many little bells and your voice. And my heart would know peace.

LAZARUS--(*tenderly*) Only a little longer! There is God's laughter on the hills of space, and the happiness of children, and the soft healing of innumerable dawns and evenings, and the blessing of peace!

CALIGULA--(*looks around at Lazarus impatiently. Then he makes a beckoning gesture to Miriam.*) Ssstt! (*Wonderingly she leaves Lazarus' side and follows him. Lazarus remains, his eyes fixed on the cross, directly in front of it. Caligula speaks gruffly to Miriam with a sneer.*) Jewess, your Lazarus is mad, I begin to think. (*then confusedly but helplessly inquisitive and confiding--bursting out*) What is it troubles me about him? What makes me dream of him? Why should I--love him, Jewess? Tell me! You love him, too. I do not understand this. Why, wherever he goes, is there joy? You heard even the galley slaves laugh and clank time with their chains! (*then with exasperation*) And yet why can I not laugh, Jewess?

MIRIAM--(*in a tone of hushed grief*) I may not laugh either. My heart remains a little dead with Lazarus in Bethany. The miracle could not revive all his old husband's life in my wife's heart.

CALIGULA--(*disgustedly*) What answer is that to me? (*then brusquely*) But I called you to put you on your guard. (*He points.*) There is death in there--Tiberius' death, a kind from which no miracles can recall one! (*He smiles his twisted smile.*) Since Lazarus will not help himself, you must protect him. I will not, for once in there I am (*mockingly*) the heir of Cæsar, and you are scum whom I will kill at his order as I would two beetles! So keep watch! Taste first of what he eats--even were I the one to give it to him!

LAZARUS--(*suddenly laughs softly*) Why do you delight in believing evil of yourself, Caligula?

CALIGULA--(*flying into a queer rage*) You lie! I am what I am! (*with grandiose pride*) What could you know of a Cæsar?

LAZARUS--(*still laughing with an affectionate understanding*) What--I know! (*As he finishes speaking all the sound of music and voices from the house ceases abruptly and there is a heavy silence.*)

MIRIAM--(*shaking her head and turning away sadly*) That is too far, Lazarus. Let us go home.

CALIGULA--(*harshly*) Sst! Do you hear? Flavius has told Cæsar. (*grimly forcing a harsh snicker*) Now we will soon know--(*There is the sudden blaring of a trumpet from within the palace. A wide door is flung open and a stream of reddish light comes out against which the black figures of several men are outlined. The door is shut again quickly. Several slaves bearing lamps on poles escort the patrician, Marcellus, forward to the arch. He passes under the crucified lion without a glance--then stands, cool and disdainful, to look about him. He is a man of about thirty-five, wearing the type mask of a Roman patrician to which are added the dissipated courtier's characteristics of one who leans to evil more through weakness than any instinctive urge. He is dressed richly. His smile is hypocritical and his eyes are hard and cold but when they come to rest on Lazarus he gives a start of genuine astonishment.*)

CALIGULA--(*who has moved to Lazarus' side defensively--in a quick whisper*) Beware of this man, Lazarus! (*then advancing--with a condescending hauteur*) Greeting, Marcellus!

MARCELLUS--(*in an ingratiating tone*) Greeting, Gaius. I have a message from Cæsar for the man called Lazarus.

LAZARUS--(*calmly*) I am Lazarus.

MARCELLUS--(*makes a deep bow--flatteringly*) I had surmised it, sir. Although I cannot pretend to virtue in myself at least I may claim the merit of recognizing it in others. (*He advances toward Lazarus, smiling, with one hand kept hidden beneath his cloak.*)

CALIGULA--(*stepping between them--sharply*) What is your message?

MARCELLUS--(*surprised--placatingly*) I am sorry, Gaius, but it was Cæsar's command I speak to Lazarus alone.

CALIGULA--(*fiercely*) And then, Marcellus? (*Marcellus shrugs his shoulders and smiles deprecatingly.*)

LAZARUS--(*with a compelling dignity*) Let him speak. (*inclining his head to Marcellus--strangely*) Over here where it is dark you will not be seen--nor see yourself. (*He walks to the darkness at right.*)

CALIGULA--(*turning his back on them, with angry boyish resentfulness that is close to tears*) Idiot! Go and die, then!

MIRIAM--(*with a terrified cry*) Lazarus! (*She starts to go to him.*)

LAZARUS--(*motioning her to remain where she is--gently*) Believe, Beloved! (*He turns his back on them all and stands waiting.*)

MARCELLUS--(*stares at Lazarus--then over his shoulder at Caligula--uncertainly*) What does he mean, Gaius? (*Then suddenly putting on a brave front, he strides up behind Lazarus*) Cæsar wished me to bid you welcome, to tell you how much regard he has for you, but he desired me to ask whether you propose to laugh here--in Cæsar's palace? He has heard that you laugh at death--that you have caused others to laugh--even his legionaries. (*A pause, Marcellus remains behind Lazarus' back, the latter standing like a victim.*) Briefly, Cæsar requires your pledge that you will not laugh. Will you give it? (*He frees his dagger from under his robe. A pause. Arrogantly*) I am waiting! Answer when Cæsar commands! (*then angrily, baffled*) I will give you while I count three--or take your silence as a refusal! One! Two! Three! (*He raises his hand to stab Lazarus in the back. Miriam stifles a scream. At the same instant, Lazarus begins to laugh, softly and affectionately. Marcellus stops, frozen in mid-action, the dagger upraised. Caligula has whirled around and stands staring, a smile gradually coming to his face. Lazarus turns, his laughter grown a trifle louder, and faces Marcellus. The latter steps back from him, staring open-mouthed, fascinated. His arm sinks to his side. The dagger falls from his fingers. He smiles back at Lazarus--the curious, sheepish, bashful smile of one who has fallen in love and been discovered.*)

LAZARUS--(*going to him, puts both hands on his shoulders and looks in his eyes, laughing affectionately--then quizzically*) Here is another one who believes in death! But soon you will laugh with life! I see it in your eyes. Farewell, Marcellus! (*He turns away from him and walks, laughing, toward the arch in rear. With bowed head the black-robed figure of Miriam follows him. Marcellus hides his face in his hands, half-sobbing, and half-laughing hysterically. Lazarus pauses before the cross for a moment--raises his hand as if blessing the dead lion, then passes below it, moving slowly on toward the palace in the rear. His laughter rises with more and more summoning power. The files of the Guard, as he passes them, two by two join in his laughter, saluting him as if in spite of themselves.*)

CALIGULA--(*sidling up to Marcellus, cruel and mocking*) Are you weeping, Marcellus? Laugh at that blundering fool, yourself! What will Cæsar say? Will he laugh when he has your body broken one bone at a time with hammers? Why did you not kill? For shame! A patrician exposed to laughter by a Jew! Poor craven! Why could you not strike? There *must* be death! Coward! Why did you not stab? (*then in a queer awed whisper*) I know! Was it not because of a sudden you loved him and could not?

MARCELLUS--(*suddenly--eagerly*) Yes! That was it! I loved him!

CALIGULA--(*craftily and cruelly*) You were about to murder him!

MARCELLUS--(*tortured with remorse*) No! No! How could I? What infamy! (*cries tearfully*) Forgive me, Lazarus!

CALIGULA--(*with vindictive insistence*) Judge yourself! (*He takes up the dagger.*) Here is your dagger! Avenge him on yourself!

MARCELLUS--(*trying to laugh*) Ha-ha--Yes! (*He stabs himself and falls. Suddenly his laughter is released.*) I laugh! You are a fool, Caligula! There is no death! (*He dies, laughing up at the sky.*)

CALIGULA--(*kicks his body with savage cruelty*) You lie! (*then suddenly kneels and bends over it imploringly*) Tell me you lie, Marcellus! Do me that mercy!--and when I am Cæsar, I--(*He begins to weep like a frightened boy, his head in his hands. Meanwhile Lazarus has arrived with Miriam at the steps before the door of the palace. As he starts to ascend these, the crimson-purple lights of the many windows of the palace go out one by one as if fleeing in terror from the laughter which now beats at the walls.*)

CHORUS OF THE GUARD--

Fear, no more!
Death, no more!
Laugh! Laugh! Laugh!
Death is dead!

ALL THE GUARDS--(*now all in a great chorus, raising their spears aloft and saluting Lazarus as if they were his own triumphal body guard*)

Laugh! Laugh! Laugh!
Death is dead!

(*Lazarus has ascended the steps. He walks into the black archway of the darkened palace, his figure radiant and unearthly in his own light. Miriam follows him. They disappear in the darkness. There is a pause of dead silence.*)

CALIGULA--(*raises his head uneasily, looks back toward the palace, jumps to his feet in a panic of terror, and runs toward the palace door, calling*) Lazarus! Wait! I will defend you! There is death inside there-- death! Beware, Lazarus!

CHORUS OF THE GUARD--(*as the laughter of Lazarus is heard again from the dark palace*)

Laugh! Laugh! Laugh!
Death is dead!

ALL THE GUARDS--

Dead! Dead! Dead!
Death is dead!

(*Curtain*)

SCENE TWO

SCENE--*The banquet hall in the palace of Tiberius--an immense high-ceilinged room. In the rear, center, is a great arched doorway. Smaller arches in the middle of the side walls lead into other rooms. Long couches are placed along the walls at right and left, and along the rear wall on either side of the arch. Before these couches, a series of narrow tables is set. In the center of the room on a high dais is the ivory and gold chair of Cæsar, a table in front of it, couches for him to recline on at either side. On this table, and on all the tables for his guests, gold lamps with shades of crimson-purple are placed.*

Reclining on the couches on the right are young women and girls, on the left, youths of an equal number.

(The masks are based on the Roman masks of the periods of Boyhood [or Girlhood], Youth, and Young Manhood [or Womanhood] and there are seven individuals of each period and sex in each of the three types of the Introspective, Self-Tortured; the Servile, Hypocritical; and the Cruel, Revengeful--a crowd of forty-two in all. There is a distinctive character to the masks of each sex, the stamp of an effeminate corruption on all the male, while the female have a bold, masculine expression. The male masks are a blotched heliotrope in shade. These youths wear female wigs of curled wire like frizzed hair of a yellow gold. They are dressed in women's robes of pale heliotrope, they wear anklets and bracelets and necklaces. The women are dressed as males in crimson or deep purple. They also wear wire wigs but of straight hair cut in short boyish mode, dyed either deep purple or crimson. Those with crimson hair are dressed in purple, and vice versa. The female voices are harsh, strident, mannish--those of the youths affected, lisping, effeminate. The whole effect of these two groups is of sex corrupted and warped, of invented lusts and artificial vices.

(The Chorus in this scene and the next is composed of three males and four females--the males in the period of Youth, one in each of the types

represented, and three of the females in similar type-period masks. The fourth female is masked in the period of Womanhood in the Proud, Self-Reliant type. They sit, facing front in their double-sized masks, on the side steps of the dais, four on right, three on left.)

Pompeia, a Roman noblewoman, the favorite mistress of Cæsar, sits at front, right.

She wears a half-mask on the upper part of her face, olive-colored with the red of blood smoldering through, with great, dark, cruel eyes--a dissipated mask of intense evil beauty, of lust and perverted passion. Beneath the mask, her own complexion is pale, her gentle, girlish mouth is set in an expression of agonized self-loathing and weariness of spirit. Her body is strong and beautiful. Her wig and dress are purple.

Tiberius Cæsar stands on the dais, dressed in deep purple, fringed and ornamented with crimson and gold. An old man of seventy-six, tall, broad and corpulent but of great muscular strength still despite his age, his shiny white cranium rises like a polished shell above his half-masked face. This mask is a pallid purple blotched with darker color, as if the imperial blood in his veins had been sickened by age and debauchery. The eyes are protuberant, leering, cynical slits, the long nose, once finely modeled, now gross and thickened, the forehead lowering and grim. Beneath the mask, his own mouth looks as incongruous as Caligula's. The lips are thin and stern and self-contained--the lips of an able soldier-statesman of rigid probity. His chin is forceful and severe. The complexion of his own skin is that of a healthy old campaigner.

As the curtain rises, slaves are hurriedly putting out the many lamps. From outside, the laughter of Lazarus rises on the deep ground swell of the Guard's laughter. The walls and massive columns seem to reverberate with the sound. In the banquet room all are listening fascinatedly. Every reaction, from the extreme of panic fear or hypnotized ecstasy to a feigned cynical amusement or a pretended supercilious indifference, is represented in their frozen attitudes. Tiberius stands, shrinking back, staring at the doorway in the rear with superstitious dread. A squad of the Guard surround the dais, commanded by Flavius.

TIBERIUS--(*in a strained voice shaken by apprehension and awe*) Marcellus! Strike him down! Stab him!

SOLDIERS OF THE GUARD--(*from without*)

Laugh! Laugh! Laugh!
Death is dead!

TIBERIUS--(*as he suddenly sees the shining figure of Lazarus appear at the end of the dark hall beyond the archway*) Gods! Flavius, look! (*He points with a shaking finger. Flavius has leaped up to his side.*)

FLAVIUS--(*not without dread himself*) That is the man, Cæsar.

TIBERIUS--Man? Say a dæmon! (*to the slaves who are turning out the few remaining lamps*) Quick! Darkness! (*He puts out the lamp on his table himself. Then as nothing is seen but the light from the approaching Lazarus*) Flavius! Stand here in my place! It will think you are Cæsar! (*He clumps heavily down the steps of the dais.*) Guards! Here! Cover me with your shields! (*He goes to the extreme right corner, front, and crouches there. His Guards follow him. They hold their shields so that they form a wall around him and half over him. Then Caligula's voice is heard screaming above the chorus of laughter as he enters the hall behind Lazarus.*)

CALIGULA--Beware of death! I will defend you, Lazarus! (*He is seen to rush past Lazarus, flourishing his sword and comes running into the room, shouting*) Cæsar! Dare not to murder Lazarus! (*He leaps to the dais and up its steps in a frenzy.*) Dare not, I say! (*He stabs Flavius with a savage cry*) Ah! (*Then, as the body of Flavius falls heavily and rolls down the steps at right, he begins to laugh, at first a clear laughter of selfless joy, sounding startlingly incongruous from him.*) I have saved you, Lazarus--at the risk of my own life--and now, hear me, I can laugh! (*Lazarus appears in the archway, Miriam behind him. He stops laughing and immediately there is silence, except for Caligula. Lazarus casts a luminous glow over the whole room in which the masked faces appear distorted and livid. Caligula stands with upraised sword by the chair of Cæsar. Suddenly his laughter cracks, changes, becomes full of his old fear and bloodlust.*)

CALIGULA--Ha-ha-ha! See, Lazarus! (*He points to the body of Flavius with his sword.*) Welcome in the name of Cæsar, now Cæsar is slain and I am Cæsar! (*He assumes the absurd grandiose posture of his imperial posing. No one looks at him or hears him. Their eyes are *on Lazarus as he moves directly to where Tiberius crouches behind the shields of the Guards. Miriam follows him. Caligula turns and stares toward him, and then down at the body of Flavius and back, in a petrified, bewildered stupor. Lazarus steps up beside Tiberius. The Guards make way for him fearfully.*)

TIBERIUS--(*feeling his nearness--straightening himself with a certain dignity*) Strike! I have been a soldier. Thou canst not make me fear death, Dæmon! (*He draws his toga over his face.*)

LAZARUS--(*smiling gently*) Then fear not fear, Tiberius! (*He reaches out and pulls back the toga from his face. Tiberius looks into his eyes, at first shrinkingly, then with growing reassurance, his own masked face clearly revealed now in the light from Lazarus.*)

TIBERIUS--(*at first falteringly*) So--thou art not evil? Thou art not come to contrive my murder? (*As Lazarus smilingly shakes his head, Tiberius frowns.*) Then why dost thou laugh against Cæsar? (*then bitterly--with a twisted attempt at a smile*) Yet I like thy laughter. It is young. Once I laughed somewhat like that--so I pardon thee. I will even laugh at thee in return. Ha-ha! (*His laughter is cold, cruel and merciless as the grin of a skeleton.*)

CALIGULA--(*who has been staring in a bewildered stupor from Tiberius, whom he thought he had killed, to the body of Flavius--quaking with terror now as if this laugh was meant for him, drops to his knees, his sword clattering down the steps to the floor*) Mercy, Tiberius! I implore you forgive your Caligula!

TIBERIUS--(*not understanding. Fixing his eyes on Caligula with a malevolent irony.*) Come down from my throne, Caligula. (*Caligula slinks down warily.*) You are too impatient. But I must pardon you, too--for where could I find another heir so perfect for serving my spite upon mankind? (*He has walked toward the throne while he is speaking, Caligula backing away from him. Lazarus remains where he is, Miriam beside and to the rear of him. Tiberius, his eyes fixed on Caligula, stumbles against the body of Flavius. He gives a startled gasp and shrinks back, calling*) Lights! A light here! (*A crowd of masked slaves obey his orders. One runs to him with a lantern. He looks down at Flavius' corpse--half to himself*) I did wisely to stand him in my place. (*to Caligula--with sinister emphasis*) Too impatient, my loving grandchild! Take care lest I become impatient also--with your impatience! (*Caligula shudders and backs away to the extreme left corner, front, where he crouches on his haunches as inconspicuously as possible. Tiberius suddenly whirls around as if he felt a dagger at his back.*)

TIBERIUS--Where--? (*seeing Lazarus where he had been--with relief--staring at his face now that the room is flooded with the purplish-crimson glow from all the lamps*) Ah, you are there. More lights! Darkness leads men into error. My heir mistakes a man for Cæsar and Cæsar, it appears, has mistaken a man for a dæmon! (*scrutinizing him--with sinister finality*) I can deal with men. I know them well. Too well! (*He laughs grimly.*) Therefore I hate them. (*He mounts the steps of the dais and sits on the couch at left of table--staring at Lazarus, wonderingly*) But you seem--something other than man! That light! (*Then he forces a harsh laugh.*) A trick! I had forgotten you are a magician. (*arrogantly*) Stand there, Jew. I would question you about your magic. (*Smilingly Lazarus ascends to where Tiberius points at the top of the dais. Miriam remains standing at the foot. Tiberius stares for a while with somber intensity at Lazarus.*) They say you died and have returned from death?

LAZARUS--(*smiling--as if he were correcting a child*) There is no death, Cæsar.

TIBERIUS--(*with a sneer of scepticism but with an underlying eagerness*) I have heard you teach that folly. (*then threateningly*) You shall be given full opportunity to prove it! (*a pause--then in a low voice, bending down toward Lazarus*) Do you foretell the future? (*trembling but with a pretense of carelessness*) Must I die soon?

LAZARUS--(*simply*) Yes, Cæsar.

TIBERIUS--(*jumping up with a shuddering start*) Soon? Soon? (*then his fear turning to rage*) What do you say? Vile Jew, do you dare threaten me with death! (*Lazarus, looking into his eyes, begins to laugh softly. Tiberius sinks back on his couch, fighting to control himself--confusedly*) Laugh not, I ask you. I am old. It is not seemly. (*Lazarus ceases his low laughter. A pause. Tiberius broods--then suddenly*) And you were really dead? (*He shudders.*) Come nearer. I need to watch your face. I have learned to read the lies in faces. A Cæsar gets much practice--from childhood on--too much! (*with awe*) Your eyes are dark with death. While I watch them, answer me, what cured thee of death?

LAZARUS--(*gently*) There is only life, Cæsar. (*then gaily mocking but compellingly*) And laughter! Look! Look well into my eyes, old Reader of Lies, and see if you can find aught in them that is not life-- and laughter! (*He laughs softly. A ripple of soft laughter from the motionless figures about the room echoes his. Tiberius stares into his eyes. In the silence that ensues Pompeia gets up and walks over to the dais. She stops to stare for a moment with cruel contempt at Miriam, then stands and looks up at Lazarus, trying in vain to attract his or Cæsar's attention. Failing in this, she passes over and sits beside Caligula, whose attention is concentrated on Lazarus.*)

POMPEIA--I admire your strange magician, Caligula.

CALIGULA--(*without looking at her*) He is no magician. He is something like a god.

POMPEIA--(*longingly*) His laughter is like a god's. He is strong. I love him.

CALIGULA--(*turning to her--coarsely*) Do not waste your lust. He is faithful to his wife, I warn you.

POMPEIA--(*She points to Miriam.*) Not that ugly slave?

CALIGULA--Yes. And yet, on our journey, whole herds of women-- and many as beautiful as you, Pompeia--threw themselves on him and begged for his love.

POMPEIA--(*her voice hardening*) And he?

CALIGULA--He laughed--and passed on. (*She starts. Caligula goes on wonderingly.*) But they seemed as happy as if his laughter had possessed them! You are a woman. Tell me, how could that be?

POMPEIA--(*her voice cruel*) He shall not laugh at me!

CALIGULA--(*tauntingly*) I will bet a string of pearls against your body for a night that he does.

POMPEIA--(*defiantly*) Done! (*Then she laughs--a low, cruel laugh-- staring at Miriam*) So he loves that woman?

CALIGULA--(*curiously*) What are you planning?

POMPEIA--I shall offer her the fruit Cæsar preserves for those he fears.

CALIGULA--(*with a careless shrug*) You will not win his love by killing her.

POMPEIA--I no longer want his love. I want to see him suffer, to hear his laughter choke in his throat with pain! (*She speaks with more and more voluptuous satisfaction.*) Then *I* shall laugh! (*She laughs softly and steps forward.*)

CALIGULA--(*concernedly*) Stop. I am his protector. (*then suddenly*) But what is the Jewess to me? (*with more and more of a spirit of perverse cruelty*) Do it, Pompeia! His laughter is too cruel to us! We must save death from him!

POMPEIA--(*walks to the dais which she ascends slowly until she stands by Cæsar's couch behind him, confronting Lazarus. But the two men remain unmindful of her presence. Tiberius continues to stare into Lazarus' eyes. His whole body is now relaxed, at rest, a dreamy smile softens his thin, compressed mouth. Pompeia leans over and takes a peach from the bowl of fruit on Cæsar's table and, taking Tiberius' hand in her other, she kisses it and calls insistently*) Cæsar. It is I, Pompeia. (*Lazarus does not look at her. She stares at him defiantly. Tiberius blinks his eyes in a daze.*)

TIBERIUS--(*dreamily*) Yes! A cloud came from a depth of sky-- around me, softly, warmly, and the cloud dissolved into the sky, and the sky into peace! (*suddenly springing to his feet and staring about him in a confused rage--clutching Pompeia by the shoulder and forcing her to her knees*) What are you doing here?

POMPEIA--Forgive your loving slave! I grew afraid this magician had put you under a spell. (*She stares at Lazarus, her words challenging him.*)

TIBERIUS--(*confusedly, sinking back on his couch and releasing her*) A spell? Could it be he laid a dream of death upon me, leading me to death? (*He trembles timorously--appealing to Lazarus*) Whatever magic thou didst to me, Dæmon, I beseech thee undo it!

LAZARUS--(*smiling*) Do you fear peace?

POMPEIA--(*harshly and insolently*) Mock not at Cæsar, dog! (*Lazarus continues to smile. His eyes remain on Cæsar. He seems absolutely unaware of Pompeia. This enrages her the more against him. She speaks tauntingly to Tiberius.*) Surely, Cæsar, this magician must have powerful charms since he dares to mock Tiberius to his face!

TIBERIUS--(*stung*) Be still! (*then in a low tone to her*) Do you not know this Lazarus died and then by his magic rose from his tomb.

POMPEIA--(*scornfully*) To believe that, I must have seen it, Cæsar!

TIBERIUS--(*impatiently*) Do you think I would believe without good evidence? I have had them take the statements of many witnesses. The miracle was done in conjunction with another Jew acting as this man's tool. This other Jew, the report states, could not possibly have possessed any magic power Himself, for Pilate crucified Him a short time after and He died in pain and weakness within a few hours. But this Lazarus laughs at death!

LAZARUS--(*looks up, smiling with ironical bitterness*) Couldst Thou but hear, Jesus! And men shall keep on in panic nailing Man's soul to the cross of their fear until in the end they do it to avenge Thee, for Thine Honor and Glory! (*He sighs sadly--then after a struggle overcoming himself--with exultance*) Yes! (*His eyes fall again to Tiberius and he smiles.*) Yes! Yes to the stupid as to the wise! To what is understood and to what cannot be understood! Known and unknown! Over and over! Forever and ever! Yes! (*He laughs softly to himself.*)

TIBERIUS--(*with superstitious dread*) What dost thou mean, Dæmon?

POMPEIA--(*with indignant scorn*) Let him prove there is no death, Cæsar! (*She appeals to the company who straighten up on their couches with interest.*)

CHORUS--(*chant demandingly*)

Let him prove there is no death!
We are bored!

CROWD--(*echoing*)

Prove there is no death!
We are bored, Cæsar!

TIBERIUS--(*waits to see what Lazarus will say--then as he says nothing, plucking up his courage--his cruelty aroused*) Do you hear, Lazarus?

POMPEIA--Make him perform his miracle again!

CHORUS--(*as before*)

Let him perform a miracle!
We are bored, Cæsar!

CROWD--(*They now stand up and coming from behind their tables, move forward toward the dais.*)

A miracle!
We are bored!

POMPEIA--Let him raise someone from the dead!

CHORUS--(*chanting with a pettish insistence*)

Raise the dead!
We are bored!

CROWD--(*echoing--grouping in a big semicircle as of spectators in a theatre, around and to the sides of the dais, one sex on each side. Caligula moves in from the left in front of them. They form in three ranks, the first squatting on their hams like savages [as Caligula does], the second rank crouching over them, the third leaning over the second, all with a hectic, morbid interest.*)

We are bored!
Raise the dead!

POMPEIA--(*with a cruel smile*) I have thought of a special test for him, Cæsar. (*She whispers in Cæsar's ear and points to Miriam and the fruit in her hand.*) And he must laugh!

TIBERIUS--(*with a harsh, cruel chuckle*) Yes, I shall command him to laugh! (*then disgustedly*) But she is sad and old. I will be only doing him a favor.

CALIGULA--(*rocking back and forth on his haunches--looking at Lazarus with taunting cruelty*) No, Cæsar! I know he loves her!

LAZARUS--Yes! (*He steps down from the dais to Miriam's side and taking her head in both his hands, he kisses her on the lips.*)

TIBERIUS--(*with a malignant grin*) Give her the fruit!

POMPEIA--(*advances and offers the peach to Miriam--with a hard, cruel little laugh*) Cæsar invites you to eat!

MIRIAM--(*to Lazarus--requesting meekly but longingly*) May I accept, Lazarus? Is it time at last? My love has followed you over long roads among strangers and each league we came from home my heart has grown older. Now it is too old for you, a heart too weary for your loving laughter. Ever your laughter has grown younger, Lazarus! Upward it springs like a lark from a field, and sings! Once I knew your laughter was my child, my son of Lazarus; but then it grew younger and I felt at last it had returned to my womb--and ever younger and younger--until, tonight, when I spoke to you of home, I felt new birth-pains as your laughter, grown too young for me, flew back to the unborn--a birth so like a death! (*She sobs and wipes her eyes with her sleeve--then humbly, reaching out for the fruit*) May I accept it, Lazarus? You should have newborn laughing hearts to love you. My old one labors with memories and its blood is sluggish with the past. Your home on the hills of space is too far away. My heart longs for the warmth of close walls of earth baked in the sun. Our home in Bethany, Lazarus, where you and my children lived and died. Our tomb near our home, Lazarus, in which you and my children wait for me. Is it time at last?

LAZARUS--(*deeply moved*) Poor lonely heart! It has been crueler for you than I remembered. Go in peace--to peace! (*His voice trembles in spite of himself.*) I shall be lonely, dear one. (*with a note of pleading*) You have never laughed with my laughter. Will you call back--Yes!--when you know--to tell me you understand and laugh with me at last?

MIRIAM--(*not answering him, to Pompeia, taking the peach and making a humble courtesy before her*) I thank you, pretty lady. (*She raises the peach toward her mouth. Involuntarily one of Lazarus' hands half-reaches out as if to stop her.*)

POMPEIA--(*with savage triumph, pointing*) See! He would stop her! He is afraid of death!

CHORUS--(*pointing--jeeringly*)

He is afraid of death!
Ha-ha-ha-ha!

CROWD--(*jeeringly*)

Ha-ha-ha-ha!

Lazarus Laughed

MIRIAM--(*bites into the peach and, chewing, begins, as if immediately affected, to talk like a garrulous old woman, her words coming quicker and quicker as her voice becomes fainter and fainter*) Say what you like, it is much better I should go home first, Lazarus. We have been away so long, there will be so much to attend to about the house. And all the children will be waiting. You would be as helpless as a child, Lazarus. Between you and the children, things would soon be in a fine state! (*more and more confused*) No, no! You cannot help me, dearest one. You are only in my way. No, I will make the fire. When you laid it the last time, we all had to run for our lives, choking, the smoke poured from the windows, the neighbors thought the house was burning! (*She laughs--a queer, vague little inward laugh.*) You are so impractical. The neighbors all get the best of you. Money slips through your fingers. If it was not for me--(*She sighs--then brightly and lovingly*) But, dearest husband, why do you take it so to heart? Why do you feel guilty because you are not like other men? That is why I love you so much. Is it a sin to be born a dreamer? But God, He must be a dreamer, too, or how would we be on earth? Do not keep saying to yourself so bitterly, you are a failure in life! Do not sit brooding on the hilltop in the evening like a black figure of Job against the sky! (*her voice trembling*) Even if God has taken our little ones-- yes, in spite of sorrow--have you not a good home I make for you, and a wife who loves you? (*She forces a chuckle.*) Be grateful, then--for me! Smile, my sad one! Laugh a little once in a while! Come home, bringing me laughter of the wind from the hills! (*swaying, looking at the peach in her hand*) What a mellow, sweet fruit! Did you bring it home for me? (*She falls back into his arms. Gently he lets her body sink until it rests against the steps of the dais. Tiberius rises from his couch to bend over with cruel gloating. Pompeia steps nearer to Lazarus, staring at him mockingly. Caligula hops to her side, looking from Lazarus to Miriam. The half-circle of masked figures moves closer, straining forward and downward as if to overwhelm the two figures at the foot of the dais with their concentrated death wish.*)

TIBERIUS--(*thickly*) She is dead, and I do not hear you laugh!

LAZARUS--(*bending down--supplicatingly*) Miriam! Call back to me! Laugh! (*He pauses. A second of dead silence. Then, with a sound that is very like a sob, he kisses her on the lips.*) I am lonely!

POMPEIA--(*with savage malice--jeeringly*) See! He weeps, Cæsar! (*She bursts into strident laughter.*) Ha-ha-ha-ha!

CHORUS--(*echoing her laughter*)

Ha-ha-ha-ha!
There is fear!
There is death!

CROWD--

There is death!
Ha-ha-ha-ha!

CALIGULA--(*in a frenzy of despairing rage, hopping up and down*)
Liar! Charlatan! Weakling! How you have cheated Caligula! (*He suddenly slaps Lazarus viciously across the face.*) There is death! Laugh, if you dare!

TIBERIUS--(*standing--in a sinister cold rage, the crueler because his dream of a cure for death is baffled, yet feeling his power as Cæsar triumphant nevertheless*) And I thought you might be a daemon. I thought you might have a magic cure--(*with revengeful fury*) But death is, and death is mine! I shall make you pray for death! And I shall make Death laugh at you! Ha-ha-ha-ha! (*in a frenzy as Lazarus neither makes a sound nor looks up*) Laugh, Lazarus! Laugh at yourself! Laugh with me! (*then to his Soldiers*) Scourge him! Make him laugh!

CALIGULA--(*running to Soldiers--fiercely*) Give me a scourge!

POMPEIA--(*running to the Soldiers--hysterically*) Ha-ha-ha-ha! Let me beat him, Cæsar! (*They group behind him. The rods and scourges are uplifted over his back to strike, when in the dead expectant silence, Miriam's body is seen to rise in a writhing tortured last effort.*)

MIRIAM--(*in a voice of unearthly sweetness*) Yes! There is only life! Lazarus, be not lonely! (*She laughs and sinks back and is still.*

(*A shuddering murmur of superstitious fear comes from them as they shrink back swiftly from Lazarus, remaining huddled one against the other. Pompeia runs to the feet of Tiberius and crouches down on the steps below him, as if for protection, her terrified eyes on Miriam. Caligula runs to her and crouches beside and beneath her.*)

LAZARUS--(*kisses Miriam again and raises his head. His face is radiant with new faith and joy. He smiles with happiness and speaks to himself with a mocking affection as if to an amusing child.*) That much remained hidden in me of the sad old Lazarus who died of self-pity--

his loneliness! Lonely no more! Man's loneliness is but his fear of life! Lonely no more! Millions of laughing stars there are around me! And laughing dust, born once of woman on this earth, now freed to dance! New stars are born of dust eternally! The old, grown mellow with God, burst into flaming seed! The fields of infinite space are sown-- and grass for sheep springs up on the hills of earth! But there is no death, nor fear, nor loneliness! There is only God's Eternal Laughter! His Laughter flows into the lonely heart! (*He begins to laugh, his laughter clear and ringing--the laughter of a conqueror arrogant with happiness and the pride of a new triumph. He bends and picks up the body of Miriam in his arms and, his head thrown back, laughing, he ascends the dais and places her on the table as on a bier. He touches one hand on her breast, as if he were taking an oath to life on her heart, looks upward and laughs, his voice ringing more and more with a terrible unbearable power and beauty that beats those in the room into an abject submissive panic.*)

(*Tiberius grovels half under the table, his hands covering his ears, his face on the floor; he is laughing with the agony and terror of death. Pompeia lies face down on the first step and beats it with her fists; she is laughing with horror and self-loathing. Caligula, his hands clutch- ing his head, pounds it against the edge of the steps; he is laughing with grief and remorse. The rest, soldiers, slaves and the prostitutes of both sexes, writhe and twist distractedly, seeking to hide their heads against each other, beating each other and the floor with clenched hands. An agonized moan of supplicating laughter comes from them all.*)

ALL--

Ha-ha-ha-ha! Ha-ha-ha-ha!
Let us die, Lazarus!
Mercy, Laughing One!
Mercy of death!
Ha-ha-ha-ha! Ha-ha-ha-ha!

(*But the laughter of Lazarus is as remote now as the laughter of a god.*)

(*Curtain*)

ACT FOUR

SCENE ONE

SCENE--*The same as previous Scene--the same night a short while later. All the lamps are out except the one on the table on the dais which, placed beside the head of Miriam, shines down upon the white mask of her face. In the half-darkness, the walls are lost in shadow, the room seems immense, the dais nearer.*

Lazarus sits on the couch at the right on the dais. His face is strong and proud although his eyes are fixed down on the face of Miriam. He seems more youthful still now, like a young son who keeps watch by the body of his mother, but at the same time retaining the aloof serenity of the statue of a god. His face expresses sorrow and a happiness that transcends sorrow.

On the other side of the table, at the end of the couch, Tiberius sits facing front, his elbows on his knees, his large hands with bloated veins hanging loosely. He keeps his gaze averted from the corpse. He talks to Lazarus half over his shoulder.

On the top step, Pompeia sits, facing right, her hands clasped about one knee, the other leg stretched down to the lower step. Her head is thrown back and she is gazing up into Lazarus' face.

On the step below her, Caligula squats on his haunches, his arms on his knees, his fists pressed to his temples. He is staring straight before him.

Only these four people are in the room now.

TIBERIUS--(*gloomily*) Was she dead, Dæmon, and was it thy power that recalled life to her body for that moment? Or was she still living and her words only the last desire of her love to comfort you, Lazarus? (*Lazarus does not reply.*) If thou dost not tell me, I must always doubt thee, Dæmon.

POMPEIA--(*with a sigh of bewildered happiness, turns to Caligula*) I am glad he laughed, Caligula! Did I say I loved him before? Then it was only my body that wanted a slave. Now it is my heart that desires a master! Now I know love for the first time in my life!

CALIGULA--(*bitterly*) Fool! What does he care for love? (*somberly*) He loves everyone--but no one--not even me! (*He broods frowningly.*)

POMPEIA--(*following her own thoughts*) And now that hag is dead he will need a woman, young and beautiful, to protect and comfort him, to make him a home and bear his children! (*She dreams, her eyes again fixed on Lazarus--then suddenly turning to Caligula*) I am glad I lost our bet. But you must accept some other payment. Now I know love, I may not give myself to any man save him!

CALIGULA--I do not want you! What are you but another animal! Faugh! (*with a grimace of disgust*) Pleasure is dirty and joyless! Or we who seek it are, which comes to the same thing. (*then grimly*) But our bet can rest. This is not the end. There may still be a chance for you to laugh at him!

POMPEIA--No! Now I could not! I should weep for his defeat!

TIBERIUS--(*gloomily arguing, half to himself*) His laughter triumphed over me, but he has not brought her back to life. I think he knows no cure for another's death, as I had hoped. And I must always doubt that it was not some trick--(*harshly*) until I have tested him with his own life! He cannot cheat me then! (*a pause--arguing to himself*) But he was dead--that much has been proved--and before he died he was old and sad. What did he find beyond there? (*suddenly--turning to Lazarus now*) What did you find beyond death, Lazarus?

LAZARUS--(*exaltedly*) Life! God's Eternal Laughter!

TIBERIUS--(*shaking his head*) I want hope--for me, Tiberius Cæsar.

LAZARUS--What is--you? But there is hope for Man! Love is Man's hope--love for his life on earth, a noble love above suspicion and distrust! Hitherto Man has always suspected his life, and in revenge and self-torture his love has been faithless! He has even betrayed Eternity, his mother, with his slave he calls Immortal Soul! (*He laughs softly, gaily, mockingly--then to Tiberius directly*) Hope for you, Tiberius Cæsar? Then dare to love Eternity without your fear desiring to possess her! Be brave enough to be possessed!

TIBERIUS--(*strangely*) My mother was the wife of Cæsar. (*then dully*) I do not understand.

LAZARUS--Men are too cowardly to understand! And so the worms of their little fears eat them and grow fat and terrible and become their jealous gods they must appease with lies!

TIBERIUS--(*wearily*) Your words are meaningless, Lazarus. You are a fool. All laughter is malice, all gods are dead, and life is a sickness.

LAZARUS--(*laughs pityingly*) So say the race of men, whose lives are long dyings! They evade their fear of death by becoming so sick of life that by the time death comes they are too lifeless to fear it! Their disease triumphs over death--a noble victory called resignation! "We are sick," they say, "therefore there is no God in us, therefore there is no God!" Oh, if men would but interpret that first cry of man fresh from the womb as the laughter of one who even then says to his heart, "It is my pride as God to become Man. Then let it be my pride as Man to recreate the God in me!" (*He laughs softly but with exultant pride.*)

POMPEIA--(*laughing with him--proudly*) He will create a god in me! I shall be proud!

CALIGULA--(*pounding his temples with his fists--tortured*) I am Caligula. I was born in a camp among soldiers. My father was Germanicus, a hero, as all men know. But I do not understand this-- and though I burst with pride, I cannot laugh with joy!

TIBERIUS--(*gloomily*) Obscurities! I have found nothing in life that merits pride. I am not proud of being Cæsar--and what is a god but a Cæsar over Cæsars? If fools kneel and worship me because they fear me, should I be proud? But Cæsar is a fact, and Tiberius, a man, is one, and I cling to these certainties--and I do not wish to die! If I were sure of eternal sleep beyond there, deep rest and forgetfulness of all I have ever seen or heard or hated or loved on earth, I would gladly die! But surely, Lazarus, nothing is sure--peace the least sure of all--and I fear there is no rest beyond there, that one remembers there as here and cannot sleep, that the mind goes on eternally the same--a long insomnia of memories and regrets and the ghosts of dreams one has poisoned to death passing with white bodies spotted by the leprous fingers of one's lusts. (*bitterly*) I fear the long nights now in which I lie awake and listen to Death dancing round me in the darkness, prancing to the drum beat of my heart! (*He shudders.*) And I am afraid, Lazarus--afraid that there is no sleep beyond there, either!

LAZARUS--There is peace! (*His words are like a benediction he pronounces upon them. Soothed in a mysterious, childlike way, they repeat the word after him, wonderingly.*)

POMPEIA--Peace?

CALIGULA--Peace?

TIBERIUS--Peace? (*For a long moment there is complete silence. Then Tiberius sighs heavily, shaking his head.*) Peace! Another word blurred into a senseless sigh by men's longing! A bubble of froth blown from the lips of the dying toward the stars! No! (*He grins bitterly--then looks at Lazarus--somberly contemptuous and threatening*) You are pleased to act the mysterious, Jew, but I shall solve you! (*then with a lawyer-like incisiveness*) There is one certainty about you and I must know the cause--for there must be a cause and a rational explanation! You were fifty when you died--

LAZARUS--(*smiling mockingly*) Yes. When I died.

TIBERIUS--(*unheeding*) And now your appearance is of one younger by a score. Not alone your appearance! You *are* young. I see the fact, the effect. And I demand an explanation of the cause without mystic nonsense or evasion. (*threateningly*) And I warn you to answer directly in plain words--and not to laugh, you understand!--not to dare!--or I shall lose patience with you and--(*with a grim smile*) I can be terrible! (*Lazarus smiles gently at him. He turns away with confused annoyance, then back to Lazarus, resuming his lawyer-like manner.*) What was it restored your youth? How did you contrive that your body reversed the natural process and grows younger? Is it a charm by which you invoke a supernatural force? Or is it a powder you dissolve in wine? Or a liquid? Or an unguent you rub into the skin to revitalize the old bones and tissues? Or--what is it, Lazarus?

LAZARUS--(*gently*) I know that age and time are but timidities of thought.

TIBERIUS--(*broodingly--as if he had not heard--persuasively*) Perhaps you ask yourself, what would Tiberius do with youth? Then, because you must have heard rumors of my depravity, you will conclude the old lecher desires youth for his lusts! (*He laughs harshly.*) Ha! Why, do not my faithful subjects draw pictures of an old buck goat upon the walls and write above them, Cæsar? And they are just. In self-contempt of Man I have made this man, myself, the most swinish and contemptible of men! Yes! In all this empire there is no man so base a hog as I! (*He grins bitterly and ironically.*) My claim to this excellence, at least, is not contested! Everyone admits therein Tiberius is by right their Cæsar! (*He laughs bitterly.*) Ha! So who would believe Tiberius if he said, I want youth again because I loathe lust and long for purity!

LAZARUS--(*gently*) I believe you, Cæsar.

TIBERIUS--(*stares at him--deeply moved*) You--believe--? (*then gruffly*) You lie! You are not mad--and only a madman would believe another man! (*then confidingly, leaning over toward Lazarus*) I know it is folly to speak--but--one gets old, one becomes talkative, one wishes to confess, to say the thing one has always kept hidden, to reveal one's unique truth--and there is so little time left--and one is alone! Therefore the old--like children--talk to themselves, for they have reached that hopeless wisdom of experience which knows that though one were to cry it in the streets to multitudes, or whisper it in the kiss to one's beloved, the only ears that can ever hear one's secret are one's own! (*He laughs bitterly.*) And so I talk aloud, Lazarus! I talk to my loneliness!

LAZARUS--(*simply*) I hear, Tiberius.

TIBERIUS--(*again moved and confused--forcing a mocking smile*) Liar! Eavesdropper! You merely--listen! (*Then he turns away.*) My mother, Livia, that strong woman, giving birth to me, desired not a child, but a Cæsar--just as, married to Augustus, she loved him not but loved herself as Cæsar's wife. She made me feel, in the proud questioning of her scornful eyes, that to win her mother love I must become Cæsar. She poisoned Prince Marcellus and young Gaius and Lucius that the way might be clear for me. I used to see their blood dance in red specks before my eyes when I looked at the sky. Now-- (*he brushes his hand before his eyes*) it is all a red blot! I cannot distinguish. There have been too many. My mother--her blood is in that blot, for I revenged myself on her. I did not kill her, it is true, but I deprived her of her power and she died, as I knew she must, that powerful woman who bore me as a weapon! The murder was subtle and cruel--how cruel only that passionate, deep-breasted woman unslaked by eighty years of devoured desires could know! Too cruel! I did not go to her funeral. I was afraid her closed eyes might open and look at me! (*then with almost a cry*) I want youth, Lazarus, that I may play again about her feet with the love I felt for her before I learned to read her eyes! (*He half sobs, bowing his head. A pause.*)

CALIGULA--(*nudging Pompeia--with a crafty whisper*) Do you hear? The old lecher talks to himself. He is becoming senile. He will soon die. And I shall be Cæsar. Then I shall laugh!

POMPEIA--(*staring up at Lazarus' face, hearing only Caligula's words without their meaning*) No. My Lazarus does not laugh now. See. His mouth is silent--and a little sad, I think.

LAZARUS--(*gently and comfortingly*) I hear, Tiberius.

TIBERIUS--(*harshly*) I hated that woman, my mother, and I still hate her! Have you ever loved, Lazarus? (*then with a glance at Miriam's body and a shuddering away from it--vaguely*) I was forgetting her. I killed your love, too, did I not? Well, I must! I envy those who are loved. Where I can, I kill love--for retribution's sake--but much of it escapes me. (*then harshly again*) I loved Agrippina. We were married. A son was born to us. We were happy. Then that proud woman, my mother, saw my happiness. Was she jealous of my love? Or did she know no happy man would wish to be Cæsar? Well, she condemned my happiness to death. She whispered to Augustus and he ordered me to divorce Agrippina. I should have opened her veins and mine, and died with her. But my mother stayed by me, Agrippina was kept away, my mother spoke to me and spoke to me and even wept, that tall woman, strong as a great man, and I consented that my love be murdered. Then my mother married me to a whore. Why? The whore was Cæsar's daughter, true--but I feel that was not all of it, that my mother wished to keep me tortured that I might love her alone and long to be Cæsar! (*He laughs harshly.*) Ha! In brief, I married the whore, she tortured me, my mother's scheming prospered--that subtle and crafty woman!--and many years passed in being here and there, in doing this and that, in growing full of hate and revengeful ambition to be Cæsar. At last, Augustus died. I was Cæsar. Then I killed that whore, my wife, and I starved my mother's strength to death until she died, and I began to take pleasure in vengeance upon men, and pleasure in taking vengeance on myself. (*He grins horribly.*) It is all very simple, as you see! (*He suddenly starts to his feet--with harsh arrogance and pride, threateningly*) Enough! Why do I tell you these old tales? Must I explain to you why I want youth? It is my whim! I am Cæsar! And now I must lie down and try to sleep! And it is my command that you reveal the secret of your youth to me when I awake, or else--(*with malignant cruelty*) I will have to revenge the death of a hope on you--and a hope at my age demands a terrible expiation on its slayer! (*He walks down and starts to go off, right--then turns and addresses Lazarus with grim irony.*) Good night to you, Lazarus. And remember there shall be death while I am Cæsar! (*He turns to go.*)

LAZARUS--(*smiling affectionately at him, shakes his head*) Cæsar must believe in death. But does the husband of Agrippina?

TIBERIUS--(*stops short and stares at Lazarus, confused and stuttering*) What--what--do you mean, Lazarus?

LAZARUS--I have heard your loneliness.

TIBERIUS--(*cruelly and grimly again*) So much the more reason why my pride should kill you! Remember that! (*He turns and strides off into the darkness at right.*)

CALIGULA--(*peers after him until sure he is gone--then gets up and begins a grotesque, hopping dance, singing a verse of the legionary's song*)

A bold legionary am I
March, oh march on!
A Roman eagle was my daddy
My mother was a drunken drabby
Oh march on to the wars!

(*He laughs gratingly, posturing and gesticulating up at Lazarus.*) Ha-ha-ha! He is gone! I can breathe! His breath in the same air suffocates me! The gods grant mine do the same for him! But he is failing! He talks to himself like a man in second childhood. His words are a thick babble I could not hear. They well from his lips like clots of blood from a reopened wound. I kept listening to the beating of his heart. It sounded slow, slower than when I last heard it. Did you detect that, Lazarus? Once or twice I thought it faltered--(*He draws in his breath with an avid gasp--then laughs gratingly*) Ha-ha-ha--(*grandiloquently*) Tiberius, the old buck goat, will soon be gone, my friends, and in his place you will be blessed with the beautiful young god, Caligula! Hail to Caligula! Hail! Ha-ha-ha--(*His laughter suddenly breaks off into a whimper and he stands staring around him in a panic of fear that he has been overheard. He slinks noiselessly up the steps of the dais and squats coweringly at Lazarus' feet, blinking up at his face in monkey-wise, clutching Lazarus' hand in both of his. His teeth can be heard chattering together in nervous fear.*)

(*Pompeia, whose gaze has remained fixed on Lazarus' throughout, has gradually moved closer to him until she, too, is at his feet, half-kneeling beneath the table on which Miriam lies, side by side with Caligula but as oblivious of him as he is of her.*)

(*Having grown calmer now, Caligula speaks again--mournful and bewildered*)

CALIGULA--Why should I love you, Lazarus? Your laughter taunts me! It insults Cæsar! It denies Rome! But I will warn you again. Escape! Tonight Tiberius' mood is to play sentimental, but tomorrow he will jeer while hyenas gnaw at your skull and lick your brain. And then--there is pain, Lazarus! There is pain!

POMPEIA--(*pressing her hand to her own heart--with a shudder*) Yes, there is pain!

LAZARUS--(*smiling down on them--gently*) If you can answer Yes to pain, there is no pain!

POMPEIA--(*passionately*) Yes! Yes! I love Lazarus!

CALIGULA--(*with a bitter grin*) Do not take pain away from us! It is our one truth. Without pain there is nothing--a nothingness in which even your laughter, Lazarus, is swallowed at one gulp like a whining gnat by the cretin's silence of immensity! Ha-ha! No, we must keep pain! Especially Cæsar must! Pain must twinkle with a mad mirth in a Cæsar's eyes--men's pain--or they would become dissatisfied and disrespectful! Ha-ha! (*He stops his grating laughter abruptly and continues mournfully*) I am sick, Lazarus, sick of cruelty and lust and human flesh and all the imbecilities of pleasure--the unclean antics of half-witted children! (*with a mounting agony of longing*) I would be clean! If I could only laugh your laughter, Lazarus! That would purify my heart. For I could wish to love all men, as you love them--as I love you! If only I did not fear them and despise them! If I could only believe--believe in them--in life--in myself!--believe that one man or woman in the world knew and loved the real Caligula--then I might have faith in Caligula myself--then I might laugh your laughter!

LAZARUS--(*suddenly, in a quiet but compelling voice*) I, who know you, love you, Caligula. (*gently patting his head*) I love Caligula.

CALIGULA--(*staring up at him in pathetic confusion*) You? You? You, Lazarus? (*He begins to tremble all over as if in a seizure--chokingly*) Beware! It is not good--not just--to make fun of me--to laugh at my misery--saying you love--(*In a frenzy, he jumps to his feet threatening Lazarus.*) Are you trying to fool me, hypocrite? Do you think I have become so abject that you dare--? Because I love you, do you presume--? Do you think I am your slave, dog of a Jew, that you can--insult--to my face--the heir of Cæsar--(*He stutters and stammers with rage, hopping up and down grotesquely, shaking his fist at Lazarus, who smiles at him affectionately as at a child in a tantrum.*)

LAZARUS--(*catching his eyes and holding them with his glance--calmly*) Believe, Caligula!

CALIGULA--(*again overcome--stuttering with strange terror*) Believe? But I cannot! I must not! You cannot know me, if--You are a holy man! You are a god in a mortal body--you can laugh with joy to be alive--while I--Oh, no, you cannot love me! There is nothing in me at bottom but a despising and an evil eye! You cannot! You are only being kind! (*hysterically*) I do not want your kindness! I hate your pity! I am too proud! I am too strong! (*He collapses weepingly, kneeling and clutching Lazarus' hand in both of his.*)

LAZARUS--(*smiling*) You are so proud of being evil! What if there is no evil? What if there are only health and sickness? Believe in the healthy god called Man in you! Laugh at Caligula, the funny clown who beats the backside of his shadow with a bladder and thinks thereby he is Evil, the Enemy of God! (*He suddenly lifts the face of Caligula and stares into his eyes.*) Believe! What if you are a man and men are despicable? Men are also unimportant! Men pass! Like rain into the sea! The sea remains! Man remains! Man slowly arises from the past of the race of men that was his tomb of death! For Man death is not! Man, Son of God's Laughter, *is*! (*He begins to laugh triumphantly, staring deep into Caligula's eyes.*) *Is*, Caligula! Believe in the laughing god within you!

CALIGULA--(*bursting suddenly into choking, joyful laughter--like a visionary*) I believe! I believe there is love even for Caligula! I can laugh--now--Lazarus! Free laughter! Clean! No sickness! No lust for death! My corpse no longer rots in my heart! The tomb is full of sunlight! I am alive! I who love Man, I who can love and laugh! Listen, Lazarus! I dream! When I am Cæsar, I will devote my power to your truth. I will decree that there must be kindness and love! I will make the Empire one great Blessed Isle! Rome shall know happiness, it shall believe in life, it shall learn to laugh your laughter, Lazarus, or I--(*He raises his hand in an imperial autocratic gesture.*)

LAZARUS--(*gaily mocking*) Or you will cut off its head?

CALIGULA--(*fiercely*) Yes! I will--! (*Then meeting Lazarus' eyes, he beats his head with his fists crazily.*) Forgive me! I forget! I forget!

LAZARUS--Go out under the sky! Let your heart climb on laughter to a star! Then make it look down at earth, and watch Caligula commanding Life under pain of death to do his will! (*He laughs.*)

CALIGULA--(*laughing*) I will! I do! I laugh at him! Caligula is a trained ape, a humped cripple! Now I take him out under the sky, where I can watch his monkey tricks, where there is space for laughter and where this new joy, your love of me, may dance! (*Laughing clearly and exultantly, he runs out through the arched doorway at rear.*)

LAZARUS--(*stops laughing--shaking his head, almost sadly*) They forget! It is too soon for laughter! (*then grinning at himself*) What, Lazarus? Are you, too, thinking in terms of time, old fool so soon to reënter infinity? (*He laughs with joyous self-mockery.*)

POMPEIA--(*who has crept to his feet, kisses his hand passionately*) I love you, Lazarus!

LAZARUS--(*stops laughing, and looks down at her gently*) And I love you, woman.

POMPEIA--(*with a gasp of delight*) You? (*She stares up into his eyes doubtingly, raising her face toward his.*) Then--put your arms around me. (*He does so, smiling gently.*) And hold me to you. (*He presses her closer to him.*) And kiss me. (*He kisses her on the forehead.*) No, on the lips! (*He kisses her. She flings her arms about his neck passionately and kisses him again and again--then slowly draws away-- remains looking into his eyes a long time, shrinking back from him with bewildered pain which speedily turns to rage and revengeful hatred.*) No! No! It is *my* love, not Love! I want you to know *my* love, to give me back love--for me--only for me--Pompeia--my body, my heart--me, a woman--not Woman, women! Do I love Man, men? I hate men! I love you, Lazarus--a man--a lover--a father to children! I want love--as you loved that woman there (*she points to Miriam*) that I poisoned for love of you! But did you love her--or just Woman, wife and mother of men? (*She stares--then as if reading admission in his eyes, she springs to her feet.*) Liar! Cheat! Hypocrite! Thief! (*Half hysterical with rage, pain and grief, she bends over Miriam and smooths the hair back from her forehead.*) Poor wife! Poor woman! How he must have tortured you! Now I remember the pity in your eyes when you looked at me! Oh, how his soothing gray words must have pecked at the wound in your heart like doves with bloody beaks! (*then with sudden harshness*) But perhaps you were too dull to understand, too poor and tired and ugly and old to care, too slavish--! Pah! (*She turns away with contempt and faces Lazarus with revengeful hatred.*) Did you think I would take her place--become your slave, wait upon you, give you love and passion and beauty in exchange for phrases about man and gods--you who are neither a man nor a god but a dead thing without desire! You dared to hope I would give my body, my love, to you! (*She spits in his face and laughs harshly.*) You insolent fool! I shall punish you! You shall be tortured as you have tortured! (*She laughs wildly--then steps down from the dais and goes off right, crying distractedly*) Cæsar! This man has made you a fool before all the world! Torture him, Cæsar! Now! Let the people witness! Send heralds to wake them! Torture him, Cæsar, the man who laughs at you! Ha-ha-ha-ha! (*Her laughter is caught up by all the girls and youths of the palace, who, as she disappears, led by their Chorus, pour in from each side of the room and dance forward to group themselves around the dais as in the previous scene, staring at Lazarus, laughing cruelly, falsely, stridently.*)

Lazarus Laughed

CHORUS--(*tauntingly*)

Ha-ha-ha-ha!
Laugh now, Lazarus!
Let us see you laugh!
Ha-ha-ha-ha!

CROWD--(*echoing*)

Ha-ha-ha-ha!
Ha-ha-ha-ha!

LAZARUS--(*moves, and immediately there is silence. He bends down and kisses Miriam and picks her up in his arms. Talking down to her face--with a tender smile*) Farewell! You are home! And now I will take your body home to earth! Space is too far away, you said! Home in the earth! There will be so much for you to do there! Home! Earth! (*his voice trembling a bit*) Farewell, body of Miriam. My grief is a lonely cry wailing in the home in my heart that you have left forever! (*then exultantly*) But what am I? Now your love has become Eternal Love! Now, since your life passed, I feel Eternal Life made nobler by your selflessness! Love has grown purer! The laughter of God is more profoundly tender! (*He looks up in an ecstasy and descends the dais, carrying her.*) Yes, that is it! That is it, my Miriam! (*Laughing softly and tenderly, he walks around the dais and carries the body out through the doorway in rear.*

(*The Chorus and youths and girls make way for him in awed silence-- then scurry around to right and left, forming an aisle through which he passes--then after he has gone out through the arch, they close into a semicircular group again, staring after him, and a whisper of strange, bewildered, tender laughter comes from them.*)

CHORUS--(*in this whisper*)

That is it!
Love is pure!
Laughter is tender!
Laugh!

CROWD--(*echoing*) Laugh! Laugh!

(*Curtain*)

SCENE TWO

SCENE--*The arena of an amphitheatre. It is just before dawn of the same night. Cæsar's throne is on the left at the extreme front, facing right, turned a little toward front. It is lighted by four immense lamps. In front of the throne is a marble railing that tops the wall that encloses the arena. In the rear the towering pile of the circular amphitheatre is faintly outlined in deeper black against the dark sky.*

Tiberius sits on the throne, his eyes fixed on the middle of the arena off right, where, bound to a high stake after he had been tortured, Lazarus is now being burnt alive over a huge pile of faggots. The crackling of the flames is heard. Their billowing rise and fall is reflected on the masked faces of the multitude who sit on the banked tiers of marble behind and to the rear of the throne, with their Chorus, seven men masked in Middle Age in the Servile, Hypocritical type, grouped on each side of the throne of Cæsar on a lower tier.

Half-kneeling before Tiberius, her chin resting on her hands on top of the marble rail, Pompeia also stares at Lazarus.

Before the curtain, the crackle of the flames and an uproar of human voices from the multitude, jeering, hooting, laughing at Lazarus in cruel mockery of his laughter. This sound has risen to its greatest volume as the curtain rises.

CHORUS--(*chanting mockingly*)

Ha-ha-ha-ha!
Burn and laugh!

Laugh now, Lazarus!
Ha-ha-ha-ha!

CROWD--(*chanting with revengeful mockery*) Ha-ha-ha-ha!

TIBERIUS--Who laughs now, Lazarus--thou or Cæsar? Ha-ha--! (*with awe*) His flesh melts in the fire but his eyes shine with peace!

POMPEIA--How he looks at me! (*averting her eyes with a shudder*) Command them to put out his eyes, Cæsar!

TIBERIUS--(*harshly*) No. I want to read his eyes when they see death! (*then averting his face--guiltily*) He is looking at me, not you. I should not have listened to your cries for his death.

POMPEIA--(*turning to him again with a shudder of agony-- beseechingly*) Have them put out his eyes, Cæsar! They call to me!

TIBERIUS--(*as if not hearing her--to himself*) Why do I feel remorse? His laughter dies and is forgotten, and the hope it raised dies--(*with sudden excitement*) And yet--he must know something--and if he would--even now he could tell--(*Suddenly rising to his feet he calls imploringly*) Lazarus!

CHORUS--(*chanting in a great imploring chorus now*) Lazarus!

CROWD--(*echoing*) Lazarus!

SOLDIER'S VOICE--(*calling from off beside the stake*) You had us gag him, Cæsar, so he might not laugh. Shall we cut away the gag?

POMPEIA--(*in terror*) No, Cæsar! He will laugh! And I will go to him! (*desperately*) He will laugh at you, Cæsar--and the mob will laugh with him!

TIBERIUS--(*struggles with himself--then calls*) Lazarus! If you hear let your eyes answer, and I will grant the mercy of death to end your agony! Is there hope of love somewhere for men on earth?

CHORUS--(*intoning as before*)

93

Lazarus Laughed

Is there hope of love
For us on earth?

CROWD--

Hope of love
For us on earth!

SOLDIER'S VOICE--His eyes laugh, Cæsar!

TIBERIUS--(*in a strange frenzy now*) Hear me, thou Dæmon of
Laughter! Hear and answer, I beseech thee, who alone hath known
joy! (*more and more wildly*) How must we live? Wherein lies happiness?

CHORUS--Wherein lies happiness?

CROWD--Wherein, happiness?

TIBERIUS--Why are we born? To what end must we die?

CHORUS--Why are we born to die?

CROWD--Why are we born?

SOLDIER'S VOICE--His eyes laugh, Cæsar! He is dying! He would
speak!

CHORUS AND CROWD--(*in one great cry*) Cæsar! Let Lazarus
speak!

POMPEIA--(*terrified*) No, Cæsar! He will laugh--and you will die--
and I will go to him!

TIBERIUS--(*torn--arguing with his fear*) But--he may know some
hope--(*then making his decision, with grim fatalism*) Hope--or nothing! (*calls to the Soldiers*) Let him speak!

CHORUS AND CROWD--(*cheering*) Hail, Cæsar!

LAZARUS--(*His voice comes, recognizably the voice of Lazarus, yet with a strange, fresh, clear quality of boyhood, gaily mocking with life.*) Hail, Cæsar!

CROWD--(*frantic with hope*) Hail, Lazarus!

TIBERIUS--Pull away the fire from him! I see death in his eyes! (*The flaming reflections in the banked, masked faces dance madly as the Soldiers rake back the fire from the stake. With a forced, taunting mockery*) What do you say now, Lazarus? You are dying!

CHORUS AND CROWD--(*taking his tone--mockingly*) You are dying, Lazarus!

LAZARUS--(*his voice a triumphant assertion of the victory of life over pain and death*) Yes!

TIBERIUS--(*triumphant yet disappointed--with scorn and rage*) Ha! You admit it, do you, coward! Craven! Knave! Duper of fools! Clown! Liar! Die! I laugh at you! Ha-ha-ha-ha--(*His voice breaks chokingly.*)

CROWD--(*led by their Chorus--in the same frenzy of disappointment, with all sorts of grotesque and obscene gestures and noises, thumbing their fingers to their noses, wagging them at their ears, sticking out their tongues, slapping their behinds, barking, crowing like roosters, howling, and hooting in every conceivable manner*) Yah! Yah! Yellow Gut! Bungkisser! Muckheel! Scumwiper! Liar! Pig! Jackal! Die! We laugh at you! Ha-ha-ha--(*Their voices, too, break.*)

POMPEIA--(*rising to her feet like one in a trance, staring toward Lazarus*) They are tormenting him. I hear him crying to me! (*She moves to the top of the steps leading to the arena.*)

LAZARUS--(*his voice thrilling with exultance*) O men, fear not life! You die--but there is no death for Man! (*He begins to laugh, and at the sound of his laughter, a great spell of silence settles upon all his hearers--then as his laughter rises, they begin to laugh with him.*)

POMPEIA--(*descending the steps like a sleep-walker*) I hear his laughter calling. I must go to him.

TIBERIUS--(*as if he realized something was happening that was against his will--trying feebly to be imperial*) I command you not to laugh! Cæsar commands--(*calling feebly to the Soldiers*) Put back--the gag! Stop his laughter! (*The laughter of Lazarus gaily and lovingly mocks back at him.*)

SOLDIER'S VOICE--(*his voice gently remonstrating*) We may not, Cæsar. We love his laughter! (*They laugh with him.*)

CHORUS AND CROWD--(*in a soft, dreamy murmur*) We love his laughter! We laugh!

TIBERIUS--(*dreamily*) Then--pile the fire back around him. High and higher! Let him blaze to the stars! I laugh with him!

SOLDIER'S VOICE--(*gently and gravely*) That is just, Cæsar. We love men flaming toward the stars! We laugh with him!

CHORUS AND CROWD--(*as the flames, piled back and fed anew by the Soldiers, flare upward and are reflected on their masks in dancing waves of light*)

We love men flaming toward the stars!
We laugh!

POMPEIA--(*in the arena*) The fire calls me. My burning heart calls for the fire! (*She laughs softly and passes swiftly across the arena toward Lazarus.*)

TIBERIUS--(*in a sort of childish complaint*) You must pardon me, Lazarus. This is my Cæsar's duty--to kill you! You have no right to laugh--before all these people--at Cæsar. It is not kind. (*He sobs snuffingly--then begins to laugh at himself.*

(*Suddenly the flames waver, die down, then shoot up again and Pompeia's laughter is heard for a moment, rising clear and passionately with that of Lazarus, then dying quickly out.*)

SOLDIER'S VOICE--A woman has thrown herself in the flames, Cæsar! She laughs with Lazarus!

TIBERIUS--(*in a sudden panicky flurry--feverishly*) Quick, Lazarus! You will soon be silent! Speak!--in the name of man's solitude--his agony of farewell--what is beyond there, Lazarus? (*His voice has risen to a passionate entreaty.*)

CHORUS--(*in a great pleading echo*) What is beyond there, Lazarus?

CROWD--What is beyond?

LAZARUS--(*his voice speaking lovingly, with a surpassing clearness and exaltation*) Life! Eternity! Stars and dust! God's Eternal Laughter! (*His laughter bursts forth now in its highest pitch of ecstatic summons to the feast and sacrifice of Life, the Eternal.*

(*The Crowds laugh with him in a frenzied rhythmic chorus. Led by the Chorus, they pour down from the banked walls of the amphitheatre and dance in the flaring reflection of the flames strange wild measures of liberated joy. Tiberius stands on the raised dais laughing great shouts of clear, fearless laughter.*)

CHORUS--(*chanting as they dance*)

Laugh! Laugh!
We are stars!
We are dust!
We are gods!
We are laughter!

CROWD--

We are dust!
We are gods!
Laugh! Laugh!

CALIGULA--(*enters from behind Tiberius. His aspect is wild, his hair disheveled, his clothes torn, he is panting as if exhausted by running. He stares toward the flames stupidly--then screams despairingly above the chant*) Lazarus! I come to save you! Do you still live, Lazarus?

Lazarus Laughed

TIBERIUS--(*has been speaking. His words are now heard as the tumult momentarily dies down.*) I have lived long enough! I will die with Lazarus! I no longer fear death! I laugh! I laugh at Cæsar! I advise you, my brothers, fear not Cæsars! Seek Man in the brotherhood of the dust! Cæsar is your fear of Man! I counsel you, laugh away your Cæsars!

CALIGULA--(*with resentful jealousy and rage--in a voice rising to a scream*) What do I hear, Lazarus? You laugh with your murderer? You give him your laughter? You have forgotten me--my love--you make him love you--you make him laugh at Cæsars--at me! (*suddenly springs on Tiberius in a fury and grabbing him by the throat chokes him, forcing him back on the throne--screaming*) Die, traitor! Die! (*Tiberius' body relaxes in his hands, dead, and slips from the chair. Caligula rushes madly down the stairs into the midst of the oblivious, laughing, dancing crowd, screaming*) You have betrayed me, dog of a Jew! You have betrayed Cæsar! (*beginning to be caught by the contagion of the laughter*) Ha-ah--No! I will not laugh! I will kill you! Give me a spear! (*He snatches a spear from a soldier and fights his way drunkenly toward the flames, like a man half overcome by a poisonous gas, shouting, half-laughing in spite of himself, half-weeping with rage.*) Ha-ha--The gods be with Cæsar Caligula! O Immortal Gods, give thy brother strength! You shall die, Lazarus--die--Ha-ah--! (*He disappears toward the flames, his spear held ready to stab.*)

CHORUS AND CROWD--(*who have been entirely oblivious of him--chanting*)

Laugh! Laugh!
We are gods!
We are dust!

LAZARUS--(*At his first word there is a profound silence in which each dancer remains frozen in the last movement.*) Hail, Caligula Cæsar! Men forget! (*He laughs with gay mockery as at a child.*)

CHORUS AND CROWD--(*starting to laugh*) Laugh! Laugh! (*Then there is a fierce cry of rage from Caligula and Lazarus' laughter ceases, and with it the laughter of the Crowd turns to a wail of fear and lamentation.*)

CALIGULA--(*dashes back among them waving his bloody spear and rushing up to the throne stands on it and strikes a grandiose pose*) I have killed God! I am Death! Death is Cæsar!

CHORUS AND CROWD---(*turning and scurrying away--huddled in fleeing groups, crouching close to the ground like a multitude of terrified rats, their voices squeaky now with fright*) Hail, Cæsar! Hail to Death! (*They are gone.*)

CALIGULA--(*keeping his absurd majestic pose, turns and addresses with rhetorical intoning, and flowing gestures, the body of Lazarus, high upon its stake, the flames below it now flickering fitfully*) Hail, Caligula! Hero of heroes, conqueror of the Dæmon, Lazarus, who taught the treason that fear and death were dead! But I am Lord of Fear! I am Cæsar of Death! And you, Lazarus, are carrion! (*then in a more conversational tone, putting aside his grandiose airs, confidentially*) I had to kill you, Lazarus! Surely your good sense tells you--You heard what the old fool, Tiberius, told the mob. A moment more and there would have been a revolution--no more Cæsars--and my dream--! (*He stops--bewilderedly*) My dream? Did I kill laughter? I had just learned to laugh--with love! (*more confusedly*) I must be a little mad, Lazarus. It was one terror too many, to have been laughing your laughter in the night, to have been dreaming great yearning dreams of all the good my love might do for men when I was Cæsar--and then, to hear the old howling of mob lust, and to run here--and there a high white flame amidst the fire--you, Lazarus!--dying!--laughing with him--Tiberius--betraying me--who loved you, Lazarus! Yes, I became mad! I am mad! And I can laugh my own mad laughter, Lazarus--my own! Ha-ha-ha-ha! (*He laughs with a wild triumphant madness and again rhetorically, with sweeping gestures and ferocious capers*) And all of men are vile and mad, and I shall be their madmen's Cæsar! (*He turns as if addressing an amphitheatre full of his subjects.*) O my good people, my faithful scum, my brother swine, Lazarus is dead and we have murdered great laughter, and it befits our madness to have done so, and it is befitting above all to have Caligula for Cæsar! (*then savagely*) Kneel down! Abase yourselves! I am your Cæsar and your God! Hail! (*He stands saluting himself with a crazy intensity that is not without grandeur. A pause. Suddenly the silence seems to crush down upon him; he is aware that he is alone in the vast arena; he whirls about, looking around him as if he felt an assassin at his back; he lunges with his spear at imaginary foes, jumping, dodging from side to side, yelping*) Ho, there! Help! Help! Your Cæsar calls you! Help, my people! To the rescue! (*suddenly throwing his spear away and sinking on his knees, his face toward Lazarus, supplicatingly*) Lazarus! Forgive me! Help me! Fear kills me! Save me from death! (*He is groveling in a paroxysm of terror, grinding his face in his fists as if to hide it.*)

LAZARUS--(*His voice is heard in a gentle, expiring sigh of compassion, followed by a faint dying note of laughter that rises and is lost in the sky like the flight of his soul back into the womb of Infinity.*) Fear not, Caligula! There is no death!

CALIGULA--(*lifts his head at the first sound and rises with the laughter to his feet, until, as it is finally lost, he is on tip-toes, his arms straining upward to the sky, a tender, childish laughter of love on his lips*) I laugh, Lazarus! I laugh with you! (*then grief-stricken*) Lazarus! (*He hides his face in his hands, weeping.*) No more! (*then beats his head with his fists*) I will remember! I will! (*then suddenly, with a return to grotesqueness--harshly*) All the same, I killed him and I proved there is death! (*immediately overcome by remorse, groveling and beating himself*) Fool! Madman! Forgive me, Lazarus! Men forget!

(*Curtain*)

Also from Benediction Books ...
Wandering Between Two Worlds: Essays on Faith and Art
Anita Mathias
Benediction Books, 2007
152 pages
ISBN: 0955373700

Available from www.amazon.com, www.amazon.co.uk

In these wide-ranging lyrical essays, Anita Mathias writes, in lush, lovely prose, of her naughty Catholic childhood in Jamshedpur, India; her large, eccentric family in Mangalore, a sea-coast town converted by the Portuguese in the sixteenth century; her rebellion and atheism as a teenager in her Himalayan boarding school, run by German missionary nuns, St. Mary's Convent, Nainital; and her abrupt religious conversion after which she entered Mother Teresa's convent in Calcutta as a novice. Later rich, elegant essays explore the dualities of her life as a writer, mother, and Christian in the United States-- Domesticity and Art, Writing and Prayer, and the experience of being "an alien and stranger" as an immigrant in America, sensing the need for roots.

About the Author

Anita Mathias was born in India, has a B.A. and M.A. in English from Somerville College, Oxford University and an M.A. in Creative Writing from the Ohio State University. Her essays have been published in The Washington Post, The London Magazine, The Virginia Quarterly Review, Commonweal, Notre Dame Magazine, America, The Christian Century, Religion Online, The Southwest Review, Contemporary Literary Criticism, New Letters, The Journal, and two of HarperSanFrancisco's The Best Spiritual Writing anthologies. Her non-fiction has won fellowships from The National Endowment for the Arts; The Minnesota State Arts Board; The Jerome Foundation, The Vermont Studio Center; The Virginia Centre for the Creative Arts, and the First Prize for the Best General Interest Article from the Catholic Press Association of the United States and Canada. Anita has taught Creative Writing at the College of William and Mary, and now lives and writes in Oxford, England.

www.anitamathias.com
wanderingbetweentwoworlds.blogspot.com (General and Culture)
thegoodbooksblog.blogspot.com (Reading and Writing)
theoxfordchristian.blogspot.com (Christian)

www.ingramcontent.com/pod-product-compliance
Lightning Source LLC
Chambersburg PA
CBHW021206020426
42331CB00003B/224